FREEDOM AND VALUE

FREEDOM
AND VALUE

Edited by
Robert O. Johann

New York
Fordham University Press
1976

Printed in the United States of America

CONTENTS

THE CONTRIBUTORS

W. NORRIS CLARKE, S.J.   Professor
                                          of Philosophy

VINCENT M. COOKE, S.J.   Assistant Professor
                                          of Philosophy

JOSEPH V. DOLAN, S.J.   Associate Professor
                                          of Philosophy

LEONARD C. FELDSTEIN   Associate Professor
                                          of Philosophy

ROBERT O. JOHANN   Professor
                                          of Philosophy

CHARLES A. KELBLEY   Associate Professor
                                          of Philosophy

QUENTIN LAUER, S.J.   Professor
                                          of Philosophy

GERALD A. McCOOL, S.J.   Professor
                                          of Philosophy

ANDREW C. VARGA, S.J.   Assistant Professor
                                          of Philosophy

FORDHAM UNIVERSITY

Preface

ROBERT O. JOHANN

IN THE FOLLOWING PAGES nine members of Fordham University's Department of Philosophy set down their reflections on the mystery of human freedom and some questions of value to which it gives rise.

Although suggested by our nation's bicentennial celebration, the theme is as old as philosophy. Right from the beginning, the idea that human development is not a matter of course but a matter of choice, that in some sense a person can fail as a person, has preoccupied Western man. Nor (what is perhaps remarkable in so short a volume) is any major period of that long preoccupation neglected in these pages. Not only are the authors conversant with a tradition which reaches from Socrates to John Rawls; they also draw upon it explicitly in developing their own ideas. In addition to those just mentioned, the dialogue includes such figures as Aristotle, Ockham, Aquinas, Hegel, Lonergan, Macmurray, Wolff, Rahner, as well as the Fordham Department. But the aim is not primarily historical. History is exploited here, not simply explored. The point of the effort is to understand, and the past is invoked only in terms of its present, and indeed timeless, relevance.

This is not to say that our authors all read history the same way or are all of one mind, any more than were the thinkers they cite. There is, I think, a marvelous variety on display here, not only of mind-sets and approaches, but of basic convictions. This became quite apparent in the year-long colloquium on freedom and value in which the contributors engaged prior to writing their essays. And one need only look at the opening and closing pieces, each of which bears on the relation between freedom and the good, to see that a reader will not be able to agree with everything in this book but will have to do some thinking and discerning on his own.

More important, however, than the inevitable and, I should say, healthy disagreements is the remarkable underlying consensus which is in evidence—remarkable, that is, for a contemporary department of philosophy. Whatever their differences of emphasis and interpretation, all the contributors are as one in their defense of man's freedom and dignity, and their rooting it in his rational nature. This is notable in an age like our own when the widespread doubts and confusions about matters of value are often enough only aggravated by the professional philosopher, and when someone in search of insight into man's nature and destiny usually finds precious little to support the view that there is anything special about him.

Also worthy of note is the way the different essays come together to orchestrate the common theme. Although, as I have said, the contributors did engage in a colloquium on the subject matter of this volume prior to writing their papers, each chose and developed his own topic in the light of his special interests and with only minimal nudging from me. What a delight it was for me, therefore, to see how well they meshed. Instead of the hopelessly random quality usually encountered in collections of this kind, this one has a notable measure of coherence. As I see it, the essays fall into three groups of three, each with a different emphasis. In the first group, the focus is on the general nature of personal freedom and the evidence for asserting its existence. Here the roots of freedom are traced and its constitutive presence in human relationships highlighted. The second triad is concerned with freedom more as a developing reality, and so the stress is on the dynamics and conditions for growth in personal autonomy. In the final group, the social context of freedom comes to the fore and, after a survey of the kinds of problems confronting freedom in the contemporary world, different philosophical strategies for approaching and coping with them are explored.

This, to be sure, is only one way of ordering the present material and, after he delves into the essays themselves, the reader may see other possibilities. My point here is not to argue for the arrangement adopted so much as to indicate its rationale. Although no collection such as this could ever do justice to the complexities of the theme it takes up, this one at least takes many of them into account and in a reasonably orderly way. It is offered, therefore, in the hope that, in this bicentennial year, it will make a positive contribution to our nation's effort at renewed self-understanding.

FREEDOM AND VALUE

Freedom as Value

W. NORRIS CLARKE, S.J.

IS FREEDOM, taken simply by itself, in and for itself, an unconditional value, or even a value at all? Or does freedom take on value only when it is freedom *for* the good? In our modern Western democratic society, and especially in our own American tradition, we are so used to speaking with deeply—and, let me hasten to say, legitimately—felt emotion about freedom as one of the primary values of our culture, about fighting for freedom, preserving our freedom as a deeply treasured national value, that we hardly stop any more even to raise such questions. Yet on the occasion of our bicentennial celebration in 1976, when we are returning to our roots to renew our understanding and appreciation of them, it is important that we as Americans, and especially as American philosophers, raise again for reflection the most fundamental questions about the meaning of this pillar of our democratic way of life. In this paper I intend to maintain that in the last analysis freedom is not an ultimate or absolute value by itself, but takes on such value only insofar as it is freedom *for* value, *for* the good.

FREEDOM FOR THE GOOD

Let us proceed step by step in our analysis. First of all, I think it is clear, at least for anyone who has a reasonably rich conception of the nature of man, that freedom as an *ontological* power or capacity for free choice, for self-determination over one's conscious actions, is a basic *ontological value*, for the reason that it is indicative of a certain level of ontological perfection in the nature of the being endowed with this capacity. For it shows forth that this being is endowed with rational self-consciousness, making him *dominus sui*, or master of himself—to use St.

Thomas' magnificently terse and pregnant description of the essential characteristic of every person—that is, giving him self-possession and self-determination over his own actions, so that they proceed from him as their ultimate responsible center and not under the domination of blind natural forces or unconscious (hence not self-possessed) instincts. By this power of lucid, self-possessing self-consciousness and self-determination, man as person participates in his own limited and imperfect way in the dimension of spiritual reality, since by it he transcends decisively, though imperfectly, the blind flow of purely material forces spread out across both space and time.

But merely to have such a power and never actually to exercise it would be to frustrate the whole meaning and finality of the power, and hence of the person who possesses it. All active powers are ordered toward, and find their fulfillment in, their actual exercise, in their "operation," as St. Thomas puts it. He never tires of repeating that the fulfillment of each thing lies in its operation: "Each thing shows forth that it exists for the sake of its operation; indeed operation is the ultimate perfection of a thing." [1] Particular lesser powers can indeed be restrained from exercise, for good reasons, without the frustration of the whole person. But not to exercise at all the radical power of freedom which constitutes the very essence of the person would indeed doom it to essential frustration.

Hence the full value of freedom consists in its exercise. And it is surely this we are talking about when we speak of fighting for, or preserving, our freedom. For the radical power of freedom which constitutes our human nature as personal is not something we can fight to attain or struggle to preserve. It is something innate in our very human nature as given to us; we can do nothing about it save to bring whole human beings into existence by the mysterious power of nature or else destroy them. But we can struggle to ensure our right to *exercise* our innate power of freedom. Hence our focus from now on will be on the exercise of our freedom.

But is the exercise of our freedom, simply taken as acting freely, without any regard for *what* we do with this freedom, a value in itself? Despite the attempts of some philosophers to elevate free action, free choice, into a kind of pure and absolute value in itself, with no roots in anything outside itself, such a position seems clearly to be, not only counter-intuitive with respect to the common sense wisdom of mankind, but also unintelligible to careful philosophical reflection. We all can give a supporting cheer to a fellow human being who says "Isn't it great that I am free?" But this does not commit us to an equally supporting cheer if he draws the conclusion "Therefore whatever I do with my freedom is great. What counts is simply to act freely, to express my freedom; how I do it, or just what I do with it, is irrelevant. The free action as such is a value unto itself." For it is clear enough that although, on the one hand, as human persons we all have the right to exercise our freedom, on the other hand, we do not have the right to do anything we wish with it; we do not have the right, for example, to commit a sadistic murder for the fun of it, just because we do it in lucid freedom.

What this implies, therefore, is that the exercise of freedom cannot be considered a value purely and absolutely in itself. Its value is determined by the value of the objects of its choice, i.e., by the ends or goals of its choice, as chosen freely. The freedom of the act is a necessary, but not a sufficient, condition for the value judgment we put on it. The primary criterion for this value judgment will be the value of the end or objective we are pursuing by our free action. And the value of these goals, in turn, will be determined by their own place in the hierarchy of values, in the order of the good as such. Hence we must conclude that freedom, the exercise of freedom, is not simply for the sake of freedom. It is rather freedom *for the good*. Freedom becomes meaningful and valuable only because it enables us to *freely-do-the-good*. Freedom, therefore, must be set firmly within the larger context of the goodness of its possible ends or goals in order to take on meaning and value in itself. Hence the true assertion "It's good to be free" must be completed by its corollary "because now I am free to do the good, to bring good into the world with the personal self-possessing responsibility which is appropriate to the dignity of the human person."

It is precisely because, and only because, of this essential subordination of freedom to the good, i.e., to the goodness of the order of ends, that our intrinsic rights to the exercise of freedom can be limited and restricted in the name of the common good, the commonly shared good of persons living together in society.

It is true that this common social good should not be blown up as some absolute higher good to which the good of individual human persons is totally subordinated. It is a limited good in the order of certain external public goods, such as peace, order of social activity, equitable distribution of goods, etc., which are in turn necessary to ensure the opportunity for proper personal development for all in the society. But precisely because it is a *common* good, and as such takes precedence over the uncoordinated goods of individual persons in these limited areas of public welfare, it can also control the exercise of individual freedoms, since the very purpose of all exercise of freedom is for the good.

It follows that a psychologically and morally healthy culture cannot be built simply on freedom as its basic value, but rather on a fundamental set of ends and goals to be freely pursued, which embody the order of the good and thus constitute the basic matrix of value within which freedom itself takes on value. But since the *free* pursuit of good goals is an essential requisite for human action to take on its full dignity and value as personally self-determined, the greatest amount of legal freedom in the external forum should be allowed for the free pursuit of these goals within the basic matrix of the common good. When we go back, therefore, during the bicentennial year to celebrate again our birth as a nation and to renew the roots of the authentic American spirit, we must be careful not to get carried away by the theme of freedom taken by itself as an absolute and celebrate it as *the* great American value and contribution to the world, without further reference to what this freedom is *for*. In a word, when we celebrate, as we certainly should with the greatest pride, our making of freedom a cornerstone of our democratic way of life, we must be sure that we celebrate, not merely freedom for itself, but *freedom for the good life*, freedom to live a life commensurate with the fullness of personal human dignity. The rootless, absolute freedom of the early Jean Paul Sartre and his existentialist followers, a freedom unrooted in value, should not be, and in fact has never been, one of the cornerstones of the authentic American spirit.

I realize that in thus taking my stand on freedom *for* the good I am entering into at least apparent conflict with the position of John Rawls in his *A Theory of Justice* and its able defense by my colleague Charles Kelbley in his contribution to this same volume entitled "Freedom from the Good." Their point is that the setting up of a framework of justice (based on fairness) in any society requires an initial (theoretical, not necessarily historical) moment of freedom *from* the good, i.e., from the inevitable pluralism of individual *conceptions* of what the good in fact consists in in the concrete. The reason is that, since such conceptions, as held by different individuals, will inevitably be heterogeneous and conflicting, the imposition of any *one* conception of the good on all, willy-nilly, will be destructive of the rights of many individuals, hence of fairness and justice. In a word, the concept of the "right" is more basic than that of the "good," and should be grounded in its own right first independently of the good. This is of course a fundamentally antitotalitarian, hence both anti-Platonic and anti-Marxist, position.

Now, I am willing to agree that in the setting up of a social order the establishment of individual rights should have priority over the *detailed* determination of what the goods to be pursued in the society actually consist in in their *material content*. Otherwise we are open to the oppression of the many by the few, although one might well argue this point further. But this is a move of *practical political wisdom* with respect to who shall *decide* what is the good in the concrete. It does not in the least weaken, it seems to me, my own more basic claim that any use of freedom must always be evaluated in terms of the choice of the good in some form or other. The Rawls thesis of the priority of the right over the good does indeed involve freedom from any *one imposed conception* of the good, but only in order to allow each one to use his freedom *for* the good which he individually claims to see. This is still freedom *for* the good in the formal sense, as distinguished from its variable material content, but with the priority given to the individual good over the common, i.e., the commonly determined, good. Yet even here it is clear, as both Rawls and Kelbley admit, that it is impossible to set up any basic framework of rights save in the light of certain "primary goods" upon which all agree, e.g., liberties and rights, powers and opportunities, income and wealth, self-respect. Although I am not too happy with all the items on this list, considering most of them either underdetermined or overdetermined, the general principle still holds: without some very general prior determination of goods the notion of "right" itself seems to lose all content and intelligible grounding. If a right is not the right to pursue what seems to one a good, it is not clear how it can be made rational at all.

THE ULTIMATE ROOTS OF HUMAN FREEDOM

Now that we have established that the basic meaning and value of all exercise of freedom is freedom *for the good*, let us move ahead into considerably deeper—and also more controversial—metaphysical territory. We must here part company with not a few philosophers and philosophical traditions which have accompanied us willingly so far. The question we are now raising is that of the ultimate ontological roots of freedom in man, from which the power of freedom itself flows—if indeed it does flow from anything deeper, as not a few deny. This general question breaks down into two more particular, but inseparable, questions: (1) Is freedom an ultimate and underivable property of human nature, just as ultimate and underivable as intelligence or reason itself, so that to say that man is rational and that man is free is to give two equally primary definitions of man (not, therefore, man is free *because* he is rational)? (2) Is the power of freedom, of free choice (if indeed these are identical, which should not be presumed too quickly), absolutely unlimited in its range, including therefore the freedom to accept or reject even the most total and complete Ultimate Good, the *Summum Bonum* or Infinite Good which is God Himself? In a word, are we free with respect to any and all possible goods, even the highest?

TWO CONTRASTING TRADITIONS

I should like to approach these questions by comparing the positions of two great families of thought within the Christian theistic tradition: that of the Thomistic school, on the one hand, following St. Thomas Aquinas, and that of the Nominalist school, on the other, following William of Ockham. The advantage of limiting our consideration to these two families of thought is that this will enable us to highlight more sharply the basic philosophical issues involved without being sidetracked by other more radical differences in metaphysical or religious world-views. For both these traditions agree on the two basic points which mark the common parameters of their discussion: (1) God is the *unique ultimate end* or final beatitude of all men; and (2) man is called to make his way *freely* toward this ultimate end, by the responsible exercise of his power of free choice. On these two points they are completely agreed. What separates them is a *purely philosophical difference* with regard to the nature of human freedom.

With regard to the first question—namely, whether freedom is a derivative from reason or intelligence as the more primary attribute and ground of the former, or whether freedom itself is an equally primary and underivable attribute—St. Thomas opts for the first position. For him freedom of the will flows from the nature of the intellect as oriented toward the unlimited horizon of being as its adequate proper or formal object. Ockham, here following Duns Scotus, opts for the second position. For them, since the intellect itself was a necessary or determined faculty, necessarily ordered by its nature to assent to the truth whenever it became sufficiently evident—a point on which St. Thomas himself agreed along with everyone else—to link the freedom of the will too closely with intelligence as its root would tend to infect the will with the natural necessity proper to the dynamism of the intellect, making it, for example, determined to choose whatever appeared as the greater good. How, they asked, can a radically free power be derived from a necessary or deterministic one?

What lay between the two sets of thinkers historically was the so-called Great Condemnation of 1277, in which the archbishop of Paris solemnly condemned a whole set of propositions (among which were several of St. Thomas') drawn principally from the necessary emanation theories of the Arabian and tributary heterodox Aristotelian doctrines which had poured into the Christian world at the beginning of the thirteenth century and which seriously threatened the traditional Christian doctrines of the divine freedom in creation and man's freedom in working out his eternal salvation.[2] After 1277 Christian thinkers became far more sensitive to the centrality of freedom in the Christian vision of the world and to the threat to it from the Graeco-Arabian philosophical traditions, and as a result tended to lean

over backward to avoid any contamination with necessary deter-
minisms either in God or in man. Thus it became more crucial
for them to proclaim with unambiguous vigor the radical freedom of man than to attempt to deduce it from any deeper metaphysical grounds beyond freedom itself.

We shall not enter here into this particular discussion, not because it is not significant and interesting in itself, but because it
would involve too long and technical a treatment. And for our
purposes the differences on this point between Thomas, on the
one hand, and Ockham, on the other, can be passed over for the
moment, since they both agreed that intelligence was a necessary
requisite for any exercise of freedom: it is in effect impossible
to make any free choice unless we first know what the possible
choices are. We shall focus, therefore, on the more crucial and
irreconcilable difference between them, which comes to a head
in the question of how wide is the range of human free choice,
i.e., to be more precise, whether our freedom extends even to the
Infinite Good itself which is our ultimate end. Are we free, even
in the presence of the *Summum Bonum*, God Himself, seen
clearly as such, even in the light of the beatific vision, to accept
it or not?

POSITION OF OCKHAM

For William of Ockham, it is of the very nature of the will to be
radically free with respect to any and every good which is
presented to it by the intellect.[3] One might say that freedom, i.e.,
willing freely, actually constitutes the very nature of the will:
freedom *is* the nature of the will. Another way of putting the
same point, in more technical language, is that the will is not a
"natural cause" at all, but an entirely different kind of cause, a
"free cause." Here Ockham is merely taking over—and in fact
repeating almost word for word—the doctrine of Duns Scotus
before him. All causes or agents, Scotus tells us, are divided into
two mutually exclusive kinds: natural and free.[4] Natural causes
act by necessity of nature, necessarily determined from without
toward their ends, as is the case with the intellect itself. Free
causes, on the other hand, do freely whatever they do, because
that is the kind of cause they are. This is their "nature," if you
will, not to be merely natural causes, but a new kind of non-

natural or free cause. Such is the nature of the will. This division of causes, moreover, is a primary, ultimate, and mutually exclusive one. There is no possibility of deriving one from the other or from anything more basic in the being of the person. Hence in particular there is no way of deriving the will as free cause from the nature of the intellect, which is a natural cause. From this follows the famous text of Duns Scotus, for which he is called a "voluntarist," and which Ockham gladly makes his own:

> If therefore the question is asked, what is the cause why the will is of itself indeterminate to this action or its opposite, or to action or non-action, it can be replied that there is no cause of this, nor is it possible to assign any cause why it thus freely elicits its acts except that it *is* such a cause. . . . Why then does the will will this object? There is no other cause save that it is a will.[5]

Hence the human will—in fact any free will—must, under pain of ceasing to be a will, remain free even when responding to the Supreme Good which is its final end or beatitude; it remains free, therefore, even when enjoying the beatific vision of God Himself.

At this point, however, Ockham parts company with Scotus. Scotus here agrees with St. Thomas that, since God is the ultimate end of the will, the total good which its whole nature is made for, the will has no free *choice* in the presence of this total Good, seen clearly in itself as such. It acts *freely*, as a will always must, but *necessarily* in this one case. Freedom and necessity here come together, since the essential note of freedom is that there be no other cause of the will's action but itself. And in this case the will embraces the Infinite Good with a total voluntary spontaneity coming entirely from within itself, without any outside compulsion, even though it does so necessarily.

Ockham, on the other hand, goes beyond Scotus to occupy a far more radical position. For him, the essence of free will is, not merely the voluntary causing of one's own action, but free *choice*. Hence even in the presence of the Infinite Good clearly seen as such, i.e., in the beatific vision itself, the human will still remains free to *choose* this good or not. Its indetermination is absolute, even with respect to its own final end.

We are here in the presence of a very radical doctrine of free will, one which makes the range of *free choice* coincide with the *total range of the good*, all the way from the lowest finite to the highest Infinite Good. Freedom, understood now as identical with freedom of choice, is conceived as one of the supreme and ultimate perfections of man—one which therefore must be present at its highest in the supreme actualization of all the perfections of man: his ultimate communion with God Himself. It would be against the nature and dignity of man not to be free in the highest exercise of his powers. This position alone, they believe, gives adequate philosophical grounding to the Christian doctrine of love freely given as the basic bond between God and man in the new Christian dispensation, based on the covenant of love and not of fear and compulsion.

Most contemporary philosophers in the personalist tradition would, I suspect, spontaneously take sides with such a position, at least with its conclusion stated above. For them, too, freedom is one of the supreme and unqualified values of human personality, and it would seem to them a scandal that in the highest fulfillment of human activity, our final beatific communion with God, the noblest thing in us, our freedom, should be abolished. So I have heard from a fair number of them when I have brought this question up.

POSITION OF ST. THOMAS

And yet St. Thomas Aquinas, who is also a Christian philosopher with high esteem for human freedom and one who makes love the form of all the other virtues, holds quite a different position; in fact, the exact opposite. For him, freedom, in the sense of free choice, is not an ultimate and absolute perfection of the person, as unlimited in its range as the will itself. It must be grounded in a deeper natural and necessary determination of the will toward the good, as concretized in God as the infinite plenitude of all goodness. And it is only in terms of this radical necessary orientation toward the Infinite Good that our wills have the power to choose freely among finite goods as imperfect participations in the Infinite Good. Our wills are free with respect to choosing finite goods as the means to our final end, not with respect to the end itself, at least when clearly presented to us as our ultimate good.

Such a position seems hardly suited, at least on first appearance, to win a popularity contest today. And yet I would like to defend it, in what remains of this paper, for it seems to me in the long run to provide a far more satisfactory metaphysical grounding for the intelligibility of human freedom. And I would add that, although it is certainly possible to hold the first position put forward in this paper, namely, that freedom is always *for the good*, without holding this second position—in fact, many do just that—still I do not think it is possible to render this first position fully intelligible unless it is ultimately grounded in the second.

Since we have no space here to undertake a textual study of St. Thomas,[6] let me present his doctrine in my own synthetic summary. To begin with, the will is an active power, a dynamism, a tendency toward. . . . But every dynamism, to have any kind of nature at all, must have some determinate orientation, some natural determination, toward some goal. To remain totally indeterminate with respect to *all* goals would make it no nature at all, literally nothing. Such a radical primary orientation to some one ultimate end, or ordered set of ends, is what defines the dynamism in question as this kind of dynamism, what constitutes its very nature as dynamism. A dynamism which is directed to nothing in particular is not a dynamism at all. An unoriented dynamism is a contradiction in terms, even in God. And this radical orientation which constitutes the very nature of the dynamism, which defines what it is *for*, cannot itself be an object of free choice, so that the active power is free to pursue it or not. It must be necessary with a necessity of nature. For if it too were a matter of free choice, this would mean that the power would remain indeterminate down to its very roots; there would be nothing for the sake of which it would be attracted to do anything at all. All choice, to be intelligible, requires some motive for the sake of which the object chosen is chosen. But under the present hypothesis we would be faced with an infinite regress in motives, since every possible motive or good for the sake of which we would choose something would itself have to be the object of a prior free choice, and so on forever. In the case of the will, it would have to be an abyss of pure indeterminate power which could never get going to seek anything in particular at all.

Let us now apply to the will in particular this general law that every dynamism must first be a nature, i.e., have a built-in necessary orientation of nature to some end or good first, before it can proceed to any particular actions. The will must accordingly be first a nature, or have a nature (*voluntas ut natura*), before it can elicit any particular acts of choice. This nature implies an *a priori*, pre-conscious orientation toward its adequate proper object, which in this case is the entire range of the good as such, since the will as spiritual faculty linked to intelligence is co-extensive in its scope with that of the intellect itself: namely, being as such, the entire range of being. The will is therefore radically and by nature, by an *a priori* natural necessity, oriented to seek the good: in a word, the will is a natural dynamism *for the good*.

Ockham might also go along this far, conceding that the will is ordered toward the good in general, but not necessarily toward any particular good in the concrete, even the Infinite. But St. Thomas would insist that we must go further. The dynamism toward the good cannot be toward an abstraction or idea. The will, unlike the cognitive faculties, tends toward union with its object in the concrete, not toward making it present in some intentional mode of idea or image. The will is strictly an existentially oriented dynamism. Now, in the concrete existential order, all concrete goods form an order of participation, such that all finite goods are good only by participation in the perfection of the one Infinite Source of all goodness, God as the Good in itself, the subsistent plenitude of goodness. Since the will seeks the good as it is in reality, we seek all finite goods only as imperfect participations of the Infinite Good. Since we are seeking the good without restriction or limitation, this means that we are really seeking for God in all else that we seek and choose as good, although we may not, of course, be able to identify consciously this total good as residing in what we call God. The will is therefore radically "magnetized" or drawn by its very nature, before any conscious decision or choice takes place, *by* God, as ultimate efficient cause of the will, *toward* Himself as Infinite Good or final cause of the will. The will as existential dynamism must be finalized toward some *existing* good as final end, not toward an abstraction.

Now, it is precisely this natural pre-conscious necessary

orientation or actualization of the will toward the Infinite Good which makes it possible for it to have free choice toward all finite goods, as partial means toward the achievement of its one necessary final end, the Good in itself. For, since no finite good can equal or measure up to the full attractiveness and drawing power of the Absolute Good which the will is by nature seeking, such a good cannot necessitate the response of the will.

It may be objected here that no finite being equals the fullness of Infinite Being which is the final end of intelligence, and yet the intellect is not free to assent or not to being as true when clearly presented to it. But note the radical difference between the two faculties and their two kinds of act. Intellectual assent to one being or truth about being never cancels out or competes with the assent to any other being or truth which is really there. Many different truths are quite compatible to co-existence in the same mind simultaneously, as long as they are all true and known as such. But the will seeks union with being, not as known, as idea, but as concrete possession of, or existential union with, the being itself in its concrete reality as good. Here a choice is required *between* goods. We cannot in the concrete be united with all finite goods at once; to have one we must give up another; we cannot be both married and celibate at once, possessing the goods of both simultaneously, nor be both a full-time doctor in New York and a full-time lawyer in Vermont. Since, therefore, possessing one finite good by its nature excludes the simultaneous possession of the other finite good involved in a situation of choice—otherwise choice itself would be meaningless, as indeed it is for the intellect—and since no finite good can verify adequately the full plenitude of the good we are seeking in all that we will, our will is not compelled by the presentation of any finite good but is left free to choose it or some other. (This presupposes, of course, that there is always some other competing pole of choice in our consciousness at the time. If in fact our consciousness should be narrowed to contain absolutely only one object as good, with nothing else present to consciousness at all as good, which it seems can occasionally happen in certain abnormal states of hysteria, etc., then we would have to pursue—not really choose—this sole representative of the good before us, since we are always already seeking the good, actualized toward the good, at all times, by our very nature. But such would definitely be an abnormal state, not a state of fully rational intellectual self-consciousness.)

To sum up: it is therefore precisely *because* we are permanently magnetized by the deepest necessity of our nature toward the Infinite Good that we are able to be free, to enjoy free choice, toward any and all finite goods along the way to this one ultimate and final Goal. It is because our will as pre-conscious *nature* is necessarily oriented toward the Absolute Good that our will as *faculty* of choice is able to choose freely between various finite goods. It is the deeper necessity within us toward the Infinite which sets us free toward the finite. All freedom, even in God, has its roots sunk deep into the subsoil of necessity, the unique necessity of the Infinite Good.

The same point can be brought out by transposing it into the more technical Thomistic language of act and potency. A will like ours, which emerges out of indetermination to make successive particular acts of free choice, is a power which passes from potency to act. But nothing can pass from potency to act save through the power of something already in act. Pure indeterminacy cannot actuate itself into determinate act. Now, in the case of a free power such as the will, whose acts are by definition *self*-determined, this principle already in act cannot be in some being outside of us; otherwise this other being would be responsible for determining us to act, and we should no longer be free. Hence in order to actuate itself to particular acts of free choice, our will—in fact any rational will—must be always already in act, permanently actuated toward some good which already includes virtually, in transcending superabundance, all lesser objects of willing. This good is the one Infinite Good which contains in supereminent plenitude all the goodness of any good we could desire. The permanent actualization of our will toward this good, preceding all particular acts of willing, contains virtually already within its power all particular acts of willing toward finite goods; for these add nothing higher to this primal actualization of our willing power which is always going on; they add only new limited participations or expressions of this primal transcendent fullness of willing the Good in itself, the Good of all goods. Hence this original, ever-present act of our will toward the Infinite is able to reduce itself to later particular and lesser acts with respect to all limited participations of this one necessary goal. Such self-determination to act with respect to finite goods is what occurs in free choice. But to be self-determining even with respect to the Absolute Good, the Good of all goods, would not make sense, since there would be no prior act to get it started. And the natural orientation of the will must be to an existential reality, not a mere abstraction.

It follows necessarily from all this that if in fact we should be presented with the Infinite Good itself, not merely in idea or abstraction or through the dark mirror of faith, but directly and clearly seen face to face in its own concrete reality *as our total good*, containing within it all the good we could ever seek or find anywhere, then we would have to rush toward it and embrace it with the total spontaneous power of our wills, as that which we have always implicitly wanted and longed for with the deepest longing of our very nature. Here the will as nature would coincide with the will as act, and the dichotomy of free choice would be transcended and left behind. For what sense could it possibly make for my will actually to be presented with the Absolute Good in itself, seen clearly as my good, what I really have wanted all the time, and yet not to choose it but to choose some lesser finite good instead, whose goodness is already contained in supereminent fashion in the original Source? Free choice here would be truly and absolutely irrational, with no shadow of ignorance or obscurity to excuse it, as we can always claim in this life to some extent. The freedom of the will would then turn out to be a dark irrational abyss of pure rootless indetermination with no relation to the intelligibility of being at all. It would be a sheer brute fact, an ultimate unintelligible surd at the heart of every rational being. The free will of man, supposed to be his supreme glory, would then become truly a definitively inscrutable paradox, beyond the reach of any access by the light of reason.

St. Thomas hastens to add, of course, that such a clear intuitive presentation of God to us in His concrete infinite reality as our total good is never and could not be available to us in this life, where the natural working of our minds is tied down to abstracting our ideas from the material world around us, accessible to us first only through the senses. In our present this-worldly mode of knowing we can indeed know God, but only indirectly by abstraction and inference from the beings of our experience, or through the partial obscurity of the eyes of faith, or through special passing gifts of mystical illumination, which always remain partially obscure. It is only by elevation to the special gift of participation in God's own direct way of knowing Himself, i.e., the beatific vision, that He could be thus directly presented to us. But if this in fact happened by the gift of God, there would then be no more place for freedom of *choice*; it would be replaced by a total, voluntary, spontaneous "yes" welling up from and giving definitive expression to the most radical dynamism of our will as nature. Short of this clear intuitive vision of God, however (not possible in this life), some finite good can appear to us with such vivid concrete attractiveness as an immediate good, in competition with the more obscure, long-range, hoped-for but not yet attainable union with God, that we are left psychologically, though not morally, free to choose the latter. In this perspective, *freedom of choice* turns out not to be an absolute and unqualified perfection, present all the way up to the supreme heights of human fulfillment. It is transcended at the highest point of our spiritual actualization by a higher spontaneity beyond all the duality and indeterminacy implied in free choice.[7]

What are the merits of this position of St. Thomas' over that of William of Ockham, together with his many modern followers, in this question of freedom? It seems to me that, of the two positions, only St. Thomas' attempts to render intelligible the phenomenon of human free choice, to illuminate it in terms of the deeper, more general laws of being and finality, i.e., of being as dynamic activity, rendered intelligible by the drawing power of the end as good. The Scotus–Ockham position, on the other hand, despite the more immediate appeal of freedom in the sense of free choice as an ultimate perfection of man demanded by the very nature of love, ends up by turning this freedom of the will into such a radically indeterminate power without roots in anything deeper that it tends to become an abyss of sheer subrational indeterminacy, beyond the reach of the light of being as intelligible. The will and its freedom, if cut off from its roots in intelligence and made into an absolute perfection in itself, seems inevitably to drift toward a pre-rational absolute of power which becomes ultimately independent of all rationality.

And it does seem clear enough that it is in this tradition of the school of Ockham, rather than in the Thomistic tradition, that certain later doctrines of will have their roots, such as Luther's conception of the divine will as absolute abyss of power more primary, it seems at times, than even the divine intelligence, and the still later doctrines of Jacob Böhme and the German idealist and mystical tradition, in which the divine will appears as a dark irrational abyss of blind power which must slowly work itself out into, or be tamed by, the light of intelligence. The Ockhamist position also stands far too close for my comfort to the much later, and perhaps unrelated, Sartrean conception of freedom as a pure rootless abyss of indeterminacy without intrinsic relation to intelligence or the good or anything beyond itself, but is a law entirely unto itself. This is freedom broken free from all roots in intelligence or being or the good, another one of Sartre's ultimate brute facts or irreducible surds in a universe ever hovering on the edge of the Absurd. At any rate, in the presence of these two great medieval traditions on the nature of freedom, we are confronted with two profoundly different and perhaps irreconcilable philosophical conceptions of the nature of human freedom (and indeed, by implication, of all freedom), which have persisted with us in some form or other right down to our own day and still remain as a perennial challenge to each new philosophical thinker to take his own stand on one side or the other.

CONCLUSION

We can now return full circle to our initial position in the first part of this paper. Although freedom as a power does show forth the perfection of the spiritual being which possesses it, the exercise of freedom can never be an absolute for its own sake but must always be, if it is to be intelligible and endowed with value, *freedom for the good*, within the context of the good. In the second part of the paper we have tried to show, following the inspiration of St. Thomas, that even *freedom of choice for the good* cannot be an ultimate or absolute perfection extending to the entire range of the good even in our ultimate union with the Infinite Good, and that it is operative only with respect to the finite dimension of the good (which includes, however, even the Infinite Good as accessible to us only imperfectly in this life through abstract, indirect, and obscure knowledge, to which we can always prefer some more vividly apprehended finite good). For freedom of choice itself is ultimately rooted in, subordinate to, and due to efface itself before, a more profound underlying natural dynamism of the will necessarily and permanently oriented—magnetized, as it were—from the first moment of its existence, toward the Infinite Good. Thus we can finally sum up: (1) All freedom, in order to take on full intelligibility and value, must be *freedom for the good, for the good life.* (2) And all freedom for the good is a secret implicit search, whether recognized or not, for the one *Infinite Good* through all its finite participations; so it is *freedom for the sake of, or on the way to, the Infinite Good.* Hence all our freedom of choice along the way is at the service of, and an expression of, a deeper natural desire for the Infinite Good in itself, and this desire is destined ultimately to flower in a supreme act of total spontaneous voluntary commitment of our whole selves to this Infinite Good, by whatever name we wish to call it (if any), in an act of freedom which transcends all duality of free choice—an act which is at once totally necessary by a necessity of nature and yet totally voluntary and spontaneous, without any compulsion from without, since by it we are now uniquely "choosing" what we finally recognize we have always really been seeking, what we have always really wanted, in all our free willings of any other good. So all freedom, in the last analysis, is implicitly *freedom for, on the way to, and at the service of, the Infinite Good, the supreme plenitude of all value.* Freedom cut off from its necessary bond with the good in the Infinite Good sinks back into a dark and bottomless abyss of irrational indeterminacy. Freedom simply for its own sake is the ultimate betrayal of freedom as an authentic value.

NOTES

1. *Summa contra Gentes,* Bk. III, chap. 113, n. 1, trans. A. Pegis (New York: Doubleday, 1956). Cf. ibid., 1.45: "Every substance exists for the sake of its operation [*propter operationem*]"; 11.94: "The operation of a thing shows forth its power, which in turn makes known [or points out: *indicat*] its essence."

2. See the standard treatments, such as that of Etienne Gilson, *History of*

Christian Philosophy in the Middle Ages (New York: Random House, 1955), Part 9.

3. See the standard treatments of Ockham, such as Frederick C. Copleston, s.j., *The History of Philosophy*. III. *Ockham to Suárez* (Westminster: Newman, 1956), Part 1; the especially fine treatment by P. Vignaux, "Nominalisme," in the *Dictionnaire de théologie catholique*, Vol. xi, cols. 748–84; and Carlo Giacon, *Guqlielmo di Occam*, 2 vols. (Milan: Società editrice "Vita e pensiero," 1941), Vol. ii.

4. See the standard treatments of the philosophy of Duns Scotus, such as Etienne Gilson, *Jean Duns Scot: Introduction à ses positions fondamentales* (Paris: Vrin, 1952), chap. 11; Bernardine M. Bonansea, "Duns Scotus' Voluntarism," *John Duns Scotus: 1265–1965*, edd. John K. Ryan and Bernardine M. Bonansea (Washington: The Catholic University of America Press, 1965), pp. 83–121; J. R. Cresswell, "Duns Scotus on the Will," *Franciscan Studies*, 13, Nos. 2–3 (June–September 1953), 147–58; Berard Vogt, "The Metaphysics of Human Liberty in Duns Scotus," *Proceedings of The American Catholic Philosophical Association*, 16 (1940), 27–37.

5. *Quaestiones in Metaphysicam Aristotelis* ix, q. 15, nos. 4–5 (ed. Luke Wadding, o.f.m. [Lyons, 1639], iv 797).

6. On St. Thomas' doctrine of free will, see, for example, Etienne Gilson, *The Christian Philosophy of St. Thomas Aquinas* (New York: Random House, 1956), Part 2, chap. 8; the especially important article of George P. Klubertanz, s.j., "The Root of Freedom in St. Thomas's Later Works," *Gregorianum*, 42, No. 4 (September 1961), 701–24, based on the fundamental research of Otto Lottin, "Le problème du libre arbitre," *Psychologie et morale aux xiie et xiiie siècles*, 3 vols. (Louvain: Abbaye du Mont César, 1942–49), i 11–389; Jacques Maritain, "L'idée thomiste de la liberté," *Revue Thomiste*, 45, No. 3 (July–September 1939), 440–59; A. C. Pegis, "Necessity and Liberty: An Historical Note on St. Thomas Aquinas," *Proceedings of the American Catholic Philosophical Association*, 16 (1940), 1–27; Gerard Smith, s.j., "Intelligence and Liberty," *The New Scholasticism*, 15, No. 1 (January 1941), 1–17. The main texts in St. Thomas himself are: *De veritate*, q. 22, a. 5–6; q. 24, a. 1–2; *Sum. theol.* i, q. 59, a. 3; q. 82; q. 83, a. 1; and esp. his later slightly more "voluntarist" texts: *Sum. theol.* i–ii, q. 8–13, esp. q. 10, a. 1–2, and q. 13, a. 6; *De malo*, q. 6.

7. *De potentia*, q. 10, a. 2 ad 5m; *Sum. theol.* i, q. 82, a. 1 ad 1m; ii–ii, q. 88, a. 4 ad 1m: St. Thomas is even willing to say that in the presence of the beatific vision we still retain what may be called our freedom (*libertas*) though not our free choice (*liberum arbitrium*).

2

Ethics as Philosophy of Freedom

JOSEPH V. DOLAN, S.J.

ONLY ON THE SUPPOSITION of human freedom—that man is in the firm sense master of his human acts, in the hand of his own counsel, and in a unique sense the originator of action—can there be a distinct philosophical science of ethics with its own formal object. Unless this be the case (and it is the office of another discipline, rational or philosophical psychology, to demonstrate it), ethics is deprived of its metaphysical dignity and only accidentally distinguished from behavioral and applied psychology. It is reduced to a system for identifying merely *de facto* "desirable" goals and the empirically effective, not normatively determined, means for their achievement. The unavoidable use of moral language and imperatives would be on an *als ob* basis, and ethics would be normative only in a diminished sense like gymnastics, medicine, or any other art. There would be recommended strategies for realizing "the good life" but no genuine prescriptions. For whatever final sense we might wring from even a morally neutral prescription to a non-free agent (e.g., "you should breathe through the diaphragm"), there can be no addressing an *ought* or *should* in their moral denotation to a subject who is by supposition unable to contravene them. For that matter, we cannot even grasp a moral concept without awareness of its implication of liberty. Justice, for example, must be understood as what is *due* another on my part as distinct from something else I may do or not. It could never be a mere result of necessitating inner forces.

It is of course possible to skirt the issue of freedom or prescind from it and still produce a fairly systematic body of ethical principles and practical conclusions, just as one may become an expert veterinarian or physical trainer without bothering about the ultimate formal or final causes of horse or man. As long as one is prepared to accept "human nature" as a given structure with its own laws of organic and psychic development and with a recognizable normality of function one is willing to respect (e.g., that honesty and bravery are *per se* and independently of consequences better than dishonesty and cowardice), one can do an amount of significant ethical reflection and reasoning.[1] It is even possible to make a formal denial of freedom on systematic grounds and yet be capable of penetrating, in-depth analyses of moral phenomena which are themselves of genuine philosophical import, such as those found in Erich Fromm's *The Art of Loving* or in J. A. Stewart's *Notes on the Nicomachean Ethics.*[2] The mind can live with contradictions which are only implicit, and for such determinists ethics has its possibility because it is judged to require as supposition only a spontaneity exempt from the sheer mechanical determinism of "physical" nature and differing from the animal's by its more extended scope. Here again ethics is but an art of manipulation which is finally univocal with the lower-level arts by which the veterinarian and gardener direct the spontaneities of the dog and tulip. There are nice dogs and mean ones; in this sense there is a canine character. But we do not speak of a canine ethics because there is no responsibility. The sorriest mongrel, given his endowment and environment, has necessarily actualized to the full his own particular potential for doghood and has nothing to answer for.

But this is not the end of the matter. The integrity of ethics as a philosophical discipline is not provided for by the mere recognition of freedom as a necessary supposition in order to get it, so to speak, off the ground. Freedom, in other words, is not finally explained as a mere condition of moral acts. It is, rather, the other way round: morality is ordered to the full flowering of freedom in that only by authentic moral activity does man finally enter into the self-realization and self-possession which is genuine liberty. Ethics is thus in the last analysis the philosophy of freedom, and awareness of this fact makes all the difference between moral philosophy and mere moralism. It is moral philosophy which must make the ultimate sense of human action, and it will succeed or founder as a practical science on the adequacy of its account of human tendency in terms of its final causes. For in practical science the end is the ἀρχή; it has the same role of principle with respect to action—conferring intelligibility—as have the first principles of speculative reason in the speculative sciences. Hence the cardinal and crucial importance of identifying the end. Without a resolution of action in such a final good—"that which all things seek"—terminating, and thus orienting, human tendency, ethics is aborted and action rendered unintelligible and "vain." A natural tendency toward a non-being is a metaphysical anomaly.

Though Aristotle, like Plato before him,[3] appreciated this psychology of action—that we cannot desire all we desire on account of something else ("for the process will then continue infinitely and desire would be pointless and vain"[4] and action itself could not ensue)—his failure to recognize the existence of will as a new and specific source of tendency in man[5] made it possible to overlook the necessity of concretizing its object in a real existent good with which man would be somehow conjoined. He saw that local movement in animals required both knowledge and appetite,[6] and that it was the presence of an intentional form in a sense faculty proportioned to its sensible object which actuated desire, there being no point to sensation in the animal other than to prompt movement toward or away from an object.[7] And he further saw that appetency in man was directed by practical intellect.[8] But the "desiring part" of the soul remained itself undifferentiated, and so he made no provision for a distinct power of tendency, a *potentia universalissima* which would correspond to an intentional form received in the intellect and account for a new kind of movement toward a good intellectually perceived. Sense cannot perceive non-sensible goods or even sensible goods universally, whereas intellect, which does, cannot produce movement. Although Aristotle realized that movement involved both a cognitive and an appetitive factor, he apparently did not get to the root of the relation, and St. Thomas' argument for the existence of a will—that to every form there corresponds a tendency[9]—completes the Philosopher on this point. At any rate, the absence of a metaphysics of will in Aristotle's psychology proved costly and leaves the *Nicomachean Ethics* on many points at loose ends. It explains why so many of the stated positions are difficult to reconcile and why one can hardly or with consistency make room for such notions as value, obligation, and antecedent conscience.[10]

While, as we have already observed, it belongs to philosophical psychology to show that man is a free agent, there are two classical arguments we should like to rehearse because they expose considerations of some pertinence to moral philosophy as well. (It will be recalled that in the *Ethics* Aristotle, like Plato in the *Republic*, explores the structure of the soul in preparation for his treatment of virtue.[11]) The first is an argument *a posteriori*, or *demonstratio quia*, which concludes to freedom from one of its signs, deliberation. Man is characteristically and willy-nilly a deliberating animal. His specific behavior is most frequently preceded by a weighing of alternative courses of action [12] before "making up his mind" (a happy formula, we may remark in passing, since, though it is neither technical nor the product of philosophical reflection, it manifests in a better and more striking way than "free will" the formal element involved in choice). Deliberation indicates that one is poised in prospect before at least two objects each of which is attracting, and to this extent moving, the will without being able to determine choice. Where the animal is, from this aspect, passively determined,[13] man must actively determine himself, and it is precisely in this that freedom consists: not *in-* but *self*-determination. True, the final or prevailing motive will be, by definition, determining, and in this sense the motive accounts for this action's being placed rather than another. Choice, to be free, must be fully motivated; if it were to be accounted for by anything else, it would be irrational, and few will argue that in order to be free, action must be absurd and out of man's control. All this is to say that it is the agent himself who determines which motive will be determining. Looking before and after and taking alternative values into his sweep, he supplies from within the values which will tip the scale. To demand more and insist that choice be free of determination by any and all motives would be to define freedom *a priori*, and with no reference to our experience of it, as a power chaotic, aimless, and irrational.[14]

These considerations bring us to a second and more essential argument, a *demonstratio propter quid*, which, in exposing the cause of freedom instead of working backward from its usual sign, yields a better understanding of its nature, "for we know a thing simply and not just accidentally when we know the cause on which it depends." Man is capable of deliberation because he is free, not vice versa. And he is free—has a power of self-determination—because he is endowed with reason, and his proper mode of action is "according to reason." He acts as reason prescribes, for, again, whatever free action is, it cannot be unthinking or mindless. There must, then, be a practical judgment guiding action. The problem is: how does this judgment emerge?

We are attracted to objects and pursue them, when we do, insofar as we find them *good*. (The tautology is only apparent; what we are saying is that there must be some *convenientia*, some proportionality, to appetite.) But everyday experience witnesses that, whatever their level of value or power to stir us, none of the particular goods proposed to us or any combination of them is simply and unqualifiedly thus convenient. One lacks what the other has; it has its price, and other goods must be forgone for its sake. Its goodness, then—the formal aspect under which it appeals—is limited and partial. And so long as vision of it remains unclouded and objective (which may not always be the case), it cannot provoke the judgment that it is simply good. We can attend to its negative aspect of deficiency, and while this state of affairs endures, there can be no necessitated practical judgment directing the will to pursue it. If such a judgment should be made, it cannot be determined by the object in the way our vision of red is determined by the rose or our judgment that radii are equal by our concept of circle. It must stem from the agent's own contribution: the *liberum arbitrium*.

An accurate conception of this extremely subtle relation of will and intellect in their mutual contribution to decision is essential for an understanding of human action in both its ethical and its psychological constitution. A first thing to note is that freedom of choice must not be taken to imply that the will is simply undetermined to start with. Quite the contrary. Indeed were such the case, man, far from being free, would be at the mercy of a lawless force in his makeup. The case is, rather, that the will, as any faculty, is proportioned to and determined by its adequate object, which is the very *raison d'être* of its existence. This original and predeliberative orientation is identical with the will's own nature as rational appetency; will is by definition a tendency toward the apprehended good or *bonum in communi*. And it is this natural tendency which makes any particular good, participating as it does in the *ratio boni*, a possible object of choice, even though, because of its particularity, it is unable of itself to determine. Somehow it must hook in with the natural activity expressing the will's innate appetite for its object.

This should make manifest the doctrinaire and ultimately absurd quality of the existentialist exaltation of freedom of choice as the absolute value [15]—a willing for willing's sake. And here we are noting only its faulty psychology. The first object of desire, from which all others spring, is the desire of a final *end*, which originates in nature, not in choice. It is therefore of first importance that the moral philosopher, who ought to understand the well-spring of action, attend to it and as far as practicable identify it and its relation to our human acts, since the end is the measure of all that is for it. Otherwise he fails to understand what ethics is finally, and, therefore, *first of all*, about. *In agibilibus finis est principium.*

A second remark has to do with intellect. That it plays an essential part in choice in the sense that choice should be enlightened goes without saying, and we have so far been considering intellect as cause or root of freedom in virtue of its power to detect the limited character of particular goods. But the enlightening has often been crudely represented and the impression consequently given that choice is the act of will alone, with intellect only externally related to it by "presenting" will with its object—this in such a way that the hitherto "blind" faculty itself, thanks to the illumination, suddenly becomes cognitive and, thus informed of the status of its object, is now prepared to accept or reject it on its own. This misconception comes from our habit of picturing mind and will not just as distinct but as separate faculties (when we do not go on to compound the error by imagining them as separate substances). Choice, however, is a composite and unified action; it is "reasoning desire or desiring reason." [16] In technical language: it is *informed* by reason, which must not only propose the end, but direct the *selection* of means as well. The desire which is choice is ordered from within, which means that the influence of reason upon it is by real inflowing through formal, not just final, causality. It guides action, not simply as a harbor light, but interiorly as a steersman guiding the ship's course toward it.[17] (This is why choice is said to be of means and not of the ends which are presupposed by it and simply *willed*; an "end" as object of choice is, as such, chosen with reference to a further end.)

But does not this involvement of intellect as a critical constitutive factor in choice bring new embarrassment? For if will is finally determined and necessitated by a practical judgment of intellect, and if intellect cannot judge an object other than as it finally appears, what has become of freedom? The free faculty is determined, and the other is not free. We may recall the Socratic doctrine that all wrongdoing results from ignorance and is therefore involuntary, since one can, by definition, will only what appears as good. The dilemma is most acutely posed in connection with ἀκρασία, or moral weakness, where the subject, apparently against his better judgment, yields to appetite. Socrates himself, from whom the problem is inherited, considered such a situation impossible. And though Aristotle disputed him on this point, even he, after a shrewd analysis of the psychology of the ἀκρατής and some refinements of the notion of knowledge, attributed the capitulation to a kind of ignorance—which is as much as to agree that so long as mind is in charge and one truly knows what one is about in the moment of action, one cannot do wrong.[18]

Here, again, the difficulty, which is that proposed by intellectual determinism, comes from our penchant to separate what are in fact mutually penetrating constituents of a single unified act. The practical judgment, of which there is question here and which is decisive for choice, is not one produced out of whole cloth and then extrinsically obtruded on will. It is itself conditioned by the will's own disposition; it could not, as we noted, with any kind of real assent pronounce an object *good* or *bad* without a cue from appetite, and so the affirmation that it is good or bad implies the will's own inclination or aversion. *Qualis unusquisque est, talis finis ei videtur*—as a man is, so the end (good) appears to him to be. And what man *is* in this context—as *doer* aiming at some good—is a function of his moral dispositions, his habits, or character. "There cannot be choice without intelligence and thought or without moral character."[19] For that matter the influence of the will extends, not only to the judgment, but even to the deliberation which prepares it, since

it itself is initiated by the agent's interest. The desires of the intemperate and the fears of the coward already prejudice their
deliberation even where they may not practically exclude it.

To understand what we may call the mechanics of choice, we
must distinguish two stages of the mind's activity. Just now we
have been dealing with mind in its most practical moment—the
judicium practico practicum, so called because it lies closest to
action which is always concrete and singular. We need, not only
a speculative–practical judgment which, though dealing with an
agibile, does so under its relatively universal aspects—e.g., that
it is good for me to study—but also one directed to me here and
now comfortably ensconced before the television set, in order to
place *this* effort of rising and applying myself at my desk. This
accounts for the perplexing possibility of two opposed convictions "in the soul" which are the condition for conscious wrongdoing: one, that it is good for me to study and separate from
television; the other, and finally prevailing one, that it is good
to remain there. The first, the speculative–practical judgment
which is the verdict of "right reason" (and thus normative), has
not been prolonged to make vital contact with the concrete movement of the will (in this instance of the "incontinent," toward the
particular sensibly appealing good) and has failed to issue in the
practical command or affirmation (which is equivalently the
choice) [20] that "study is good" at the precise point where it must
be so evaluated and affirmed if it is to terminate in action, "for
mind does not move without appetite."

Why has it been aborted? Because it has not managed to sur-
mount desire. To direct action effectively, mind must reach to
the singular, and for this it must connect with appetite since sin-
gulars *in quibus sunt actiones* are its special province. But for a
singular object to appear and appeal as concrete good, it must
find some resonance in appetite, and this supposes that appetite
must have been disposed in advance by some kind of discipline.
That is to say, for all its essentially arational quality, appetite
can "partake" of reason "as one would listen to a father." [21] And
there's the rub. In the case of conscious wrongdoing, the concrete
good which finally determines choice is the one recommended by
appetite alone and unruled and thus able to deflect the judgment
of reason (the *scientia universalis*) from concluding to a right
particular judgment or choice. When it comes to the critical

point of ordering concrete action, reason has yielded to the tug
of desire as a harried parent to the persistence of an unruly child.
It is this kind of "knowledge"—knowledge in action (what
Aristotle calls "sensory" as distinct from knowledge proper or
ἐπιστήμη) [22] which is "dragged about by passion."

With this understanding of choice as a unified act of intellect
and will, we can now consider three related personality factors
whose influence on action is often judged, not only to modify
freedom of choice, but to be incompatible with it. They are
(a) subconscious motivation, (b) temperament, understood as
the original psychosomatic endowment, and (c) character or the
stamp given the personality through acquired habits of thought
and conduct. Before considering them separately, however, we
must make a general remark to help focus the issue and obviate
some confusions likely to arise in estimating the extent of their
freedom-inhibiting influence.

A distinction must be made between freedom, or liberty, as an
achieved state of self-possession and self-disposition implying
full possession of the intellectual and moral virtues, and the freedom we exercise in individual acts of choosing which, when they
themselves are good, are the means by which we achieve it. Depending on the degree to which the virtues are present as operative habits shaping the practical judgment, the freedom which
should ideally qualify these acts may be more or less perfectly
realized. Traditional ethics has always recognized that ignorance and antecedent passion (understood as any prominent movement of sense appetite) can modify voluntareity to the extent
that they affect the clarity of the practical judgment. We are
here concerned with the freedom of individual *acts*, and it is our
position that even where, because of ignorance or appetite, perfect clarity of vision is obscured and freedom proportionately
diminished, still, thanks to the connatural perception of the basic
moral values expressed in the so-called primary principles of
natural law (e.g., justice, courage, honesty) and the will's political power over the sense appetite and imagination, it is not the
ordinary case that the operation of these rational faculties should
be so completely impeded as to destroy freedom utterly and an-
nul personal responsibility. Should this stance appear overly
dogmatic and aprioristic, we hasten to add that we are setting
no limits to the possibilities of moral aberrancy and dehumani-

zation (terms in themselves revealing), and one may grant the
existence *ut in paucioribus* of moral as well as intellectual cre-
tinism. But we are talking now about men. Men who have no
natural awareness of justice, honesty, and courage as *bona prose-
quenda* or of their correlative disvalues—injustice, dishonesty,
and cowardice—as *mala vitanda* are in the real sense "mon-
strous." And it is not good methodology to refer to the extraor-
dinary instance (if "abnormal" and "pathological" are out of
order) for our understanding of a type—in the present case,
human.

(*a*) The subconscious motive first. By it we understand principally one associated with the common sort of defense mecha-
nisms such as rationalization, repression, projection, and com-
pensation with which dynamic and abnormal psychology are
familiar. Their presence to some extent even in the normal personality we may take as established. We prefer the term *subconscious* to *unconscious* as connoting better the element of concealment and active disguise or repression. A motive can be
unconscious in the sense of not being actually adverted to for the
innocent reason that one's value responses have become habitual
or "second nature." Even were it brought to the level of conscious awareness, it would still be sanctioned; it has been "su-
peractualized" and integrated with the personality in a way in
which the subconscious factor has not. This latter, in fact, is
judged to exclude freedom precisely as constituting a lurking
force *a tergo* which is not just latent but alien. (Similarly, one
may also be unaware of the influence of one's own temperament
and character, but these, too, may be said to represent the "self"
as a principle of real spontaneity.)

What is the bearing of a subconscious motive on action? Although we will not now quarrel with this established term, it
must be noted that we are not dealing with motivation in its
proper sense at all. Though it has its own dynamics, the significant and surprisingly unremarked fact is that so long as the motive remains subconscious, no action can result. And since the
agent, whom we suppose not to be a formal hypocrite, must actively conceal his "real" motive (e.g., revenge) from *himself*
and then, again unconsciously, dissimulate it as "vindication of
justice" in order to act, it should be evident that the latter, the
one in the forefront of consciousness, does exercise, however
tenuously, a real final causality as motive.

Certainly there is self-deception involved and, to the extent intellect has been duped through the machinations of appetite, a seriously diminished freedom. It is because of a defect of the moral order (i.e., pertaining to appetite)—a kind of Sartrean bad faith for which one may or may not be finally accountable—that such forces are at work undetected in the psyche. It is thus an important contribution of psychology to ethics, as a practical science aimed at integrating the person, to have brought the influence of the subconscious to our attention. But if we are not to yield to the *ignava ratio* which would abdicate all responsibility for action, it is even more important to recognize that its operation does not immediately exclude freedom of choice in one's particular acts so as to reduce it to zero. The very resort to subterfuge shows that *some* power of self-determination remains.[23] The threat to freedom is at the deeper level of personality, and it is man's immediate task as moral agent who has to "issue a first and final edition of himself" to use his initial freedom of choice to extend the sphere of liberty to that deeper level of his being to expose and disperse all dis-integrating forces. Subconscious motives are not so utterly disguised as to escape all detection; otherwise they would not be so neatly catalogued. And they can be brought to the subject's own notice through such means as intelligent and diligent examination of the conscience, the "fraternal correction" of a friend and the advice of counselor or director who are in better position to detect and reveal them (e.g., by pointing out how a person does the same things which anger him in others, or is indulgent with the same faults in some which stir his indignation in another).

(*b*) Temperament and character we can treat for the most part conjointly. They are so evidently related as often to be taken to be the same thing, inasmuch as both include the complex of mental, emotional, and moral qualities manifested in the comportment. It is important that they be distinguished, however, if only because they stand in different relation to freedom and found different arguments for determinism. Temperament is an initial endowment and the biological basis of character. It is the stuff or, as the etymology indicates, the mixture of elements which the subject has to shape and to which character stands as final product of habitual conduct. Character thus supposes the passage of time and a personal input—or the absence of it, since one may simply drift with the temperament. This difference comes through in our use of the term "temperamental" to describe one whose actions are capricious, unpredictable, and unorganized by a controlling principle or rational habit.

There can be no questioning the general pronounced influence of the temperament on character. That there is nothing simplistic in the Scholastics' conception of freedom, based though it is on the spirituality of intellect and will, is evident from their realistic appreciation of the individual's particular biological constitution, the *complexio naturalis*, as a formative and conditioning element of character disposing *statim a nativitate* to a relatively difficult or easy acquisition of vice or virtue.[24] Certain avenues of development are opened or excluded from the start by the presence or absence of specific physical qualities. A boy's rugged frame can favor aggressiveness and self-confidence in encounters which provide the natural material foundation for the moral virtue of courage whereas an asthenic one may discourage from confrontation and promote a tendency to shyness and acquiescence. It will, *ceteris paribus*, be easier for the one and harder for the other to stand his ground under serious challege.

This is the basic reason why our early moral training is of critical importance. Nature likes to deploy itself in activity which accords with its disposition; healthy puppies, kittens, and children are not by election frisky. But a human temperament left untrammeled will prove a formidable handicap when the moment arrives (as it never will for the puppy) for a responsible and enlightened exercise of freedom. The inclination of appetite is toward the pleasant and away from the painful and difficult—a bias quickly confirmed by habit as second nature. *Consuetudo vertitur in naturam.* Unless the inclinations are marshaled early under the political control of the will, with the help of a surrogate reason in the form of wise parental guidance and the quiet pressure of the civil community through its own laws,[25] reason ("that small part of the soul"[26]), instead of taking charge as "rightful ruler" over the appetitive ("that largest part in each and by nature insatiable"[27]), will be confronted by στάσις:[28] factions and seditions within its own city and a mob in revolt.

It should be noticed that this subversion is accomplished, not through direct immediate interference with the will's executive power, but by manipulation of the practical judgment. The concrete circumstances in which actions take place will usually involve different appetites at once in subtly different ways, and unless they are well ordered, an avenue is open for infiltrating the judgment of prudence. That is why the moral virtues are interconnected and interdependent in a way in which intellectual skills are not.[29] A good metaphysician may be poor at figures and a coward besides. The coward may be expert in mathematics. But his judgment will defect in situations which arouse fear, and fear in turn will obscure his perception of what it is *just* to do when danger threatens, just as will the appetite of the intemperate where just or courageous action would mean forgoing his pleasure. Shakespeare has given us a fine analysis *ad mentem Aristotelis* of the corrosive influence of the tragic flaw:

> So, oft it chances in particular men,
> That for some vicious mole of nature in them,
> As, in their birth,—wherein they are not guilty,
> Since nature cannot choose his origin,—
> By the o'ergrowth of some complexion,
> Oft breaking down the pales and forts of reason,
> Or by some habit that too much o'er-leavens
> The form of plausive manners; that these men,
> Carrying, I say, the stamp of one defect,
> Being nature's livery, or fortune's star,
> Their virtues else, be they as pure as grace,
> As infinite as man may undergo,
> Shall in the general censure take corruption
> From that particular fault. . . .[30]

Aristotle has remarked the difficulty of hitting the mean and the great ease of missing it. Two further facts about the psychology of temperament may be mentioned to point up the delicacy of the task of moral education and the need for discernment on the part of the parents especially. They must know their own child since, unlike the legislators who direct a general multitude generally and for the common good, they must rule an individual for his own good through the personally perceptive *paternus sermo*. The first is that the same disposition which favors one virtue, e.g., mildness with respect to obedience, can make relatively difficult the acquisition of another like fortitude whose object is a *bonum arduum* and whose material component is what Plato called the "spirited" element or what will be later

known as the irascible as distinct from the concupiscible appetite. These two, as Plato also noticed, inhibit each other; if a
person is angry, he cannot enjoy the food he is eating. So effort
is needed to moderate the proclivity of the predominant element
and compensate for the weaker that both may be at the ready
service of reason.

Second, and equally important, is the fact that while a good
natural disposition is in itself a great advantage, it cannot suffice
to guarantee even the virtue it favors. On the contrary. Unless
it is assimilated to reason, "by some habit that too much o'er-
leavens the form of plausive manners," it will become destructive.[31] Popular estimates of the he-man do not represent him as
always or prominently temperate and chaste; at least we do not
list temperance first among the virile virtues. Yet such a one
should find it relatively easy to be temperate. Since he keeps his
poise in the face of danger to life and limb, he could be expected
a fortiori to despise the relatively minor pains of thwarted appetite. But if he is not formally brave—i.e., with the commitment to the *bonum honestum* which we find in our Western hero
at his finest—he has no motive to curb desire and instead puts his
"natural virtue" to work in swathing a path through obstacles
and brushing aside his weaker rivals. Thus his natural fortitude
will make him intemperate and unjust, and intemperance can in
time corrupt his fortitude. When Cleopatra turns her ships away
from the battle at Actium, Antony who once "could quail and
quake the orb," has no will left for the fight. His "heart tied to
her rudder by the strings,"

> The noble ruin of her magic, Antony,
> Claps on his sea-wing, and like a doting mallard,
> Leaving the fight in height, flies after her.
> I never saw an action of such shame;
> Experience, manhood, honour, ne'er before
> Did violate so itself.[32]

It is during what are aptly called the formative years of childhood, puberty, and adolescence that the temperament and its
management will have the most pronounced impact as it is gradually transformed into character. Long before the capacity for
moral evaluations is actualized, sense appetites together with
the imagination will have been engaged by sensible objects ap-

prehended as good or evil on the sole basis of pleasure and pain
and without reference to any moral norm.[33] A child's ends are
pretty much those of an innocent animal, and ends provide the
first principles of the practical syllogism. It is, then, a costly
injustice to himself and to the civil society he is destined to
join to leave a young person as yet inexperienced in genuine
values (intellectual, cultural, aesthetic, moral, religious) to his
own resources and to "discover his own values for himself." He
is thus deprived of his rightful patrimony. True, nature has its
resources and recuperative powers and, as a last resort, there is
synderesis, the "spark of conscience," on which to build. But
normal exercise of freedom supposes a normal environment, and
man is a political animal whose normal development supposes
the contribution of the two basic natural societies: the family to
"gentle" *per viam amoris* and the city to "civilize" through its
disciplina legum.[34] If these supportive agents do their tasks
well, temperament for the most part will have been wisely managed to become the servant of reason and liberty.

> A child's first infant consciousness is that of pleasure and pain;
> this is the domain wherein the soul first acquires virtue or vice.
> For wisdom and assured true conviction, a man is fortunate if he
> acquires them even on the verge of old age, and, in every case, he
> that possesses them with all their attendant blessings has come to
> the full stature of man. By education, then, I mean goodness in the
> form in which it is first acquired by a child. In fact, if pleasure
> and liking, pain and dislike, are formed in the soul on right lines
> before the age of understanding is reached, and when that age
> is attained, these feelings are in concord with understanding,
> thanks to early discipline in appropriate habits—this concord,
> regarded as a whole, is virtue. But if you consider the one factor
> in it, the rightly disciplined state of pleasures and pains whereby
> a man, from his first beginnings on, will abhor what he should
> abhor and relish what he should relish—if you isolate this factor
> and call it education, you will be giving it its true name.[35]

(c) Greek ethical theory had little reason to address itself to
the problems of free will and responsibility as we have come to
understand these terms today. The Greek inhabited a world
which owed its existence to sheer necessity, not to any act of creation. Nor, however much the gods might arbitrarily meddle in
its affairs, was it guided by a Providence whose ways were to be

justified. Man was the unwitting tool of passion and fate. The happiness he pursued, though partly of his own effecting, was, as Aristotle himself conceded, largely a matter of fortune. It was beyond the reach and hopes of most; it was secured in this world or never and in any case was only precariously held. In many respects morality was conceived on the model of art. While action, to be good, had to be intended for the right motive, no special value attached to it as free—as having the person at its source in a way different from the relation of the artist to his opus. Its whole worth lay in its power to effect the good aimed at. The Greek word for virtue, ἀρετή, has the primary meaning of excellence of any kind. Virtue, like art, was a matter of *skill*. And there were failures in life as there were in art.

With the advent of Christianity and a new conception of cosmos and person, it became necessary to vindicate a genuine freedom and responsibility for man. One obvious reason for this was the Christian doctrine of personal immortality with salvation to be won or lost for eternity depending on the individual's own merits. But a more specific occasion for probing and sharpening ideas was the Pelagian heresy, which forced the effort to compose man's freedom with the need for "healing grace" (*gratia sanans*) to assist a wounded nature, and with the Pauline teaching on predestination. The *De libero arbitrio* and *De predestinatione sanctorum* of St. Augustine are but two of the monuments of this formidable enterprise.

The ancients were satisfied with less demanding notions. A man was judged responsible for whatever acts he placed without coercion and with knowledge of the circumstances. He had only to know *what* he was doing. Formally evil action was action placed for the wrong *end* and that kind of error did not excuse. It stemmed from character (ἠθικῆς ἕξεως), and a man's character was precisely himself. The action was therefore truly his own and indicated his evil status as man. His ends were evil because that was the kind of man he was.

When Aristotle has to meet the Socratic objection which would eliminate responsibility for evil action on the ground that one does not willingly do wrong and one cannot help seeing things as one does, his answer is that while our estimate of the good does in fact depend on our character, we are still responsible because we were able previously to avoid the evil actions which finally produced it. That these latter are truly in our power is shown from the practice of encouraging and dissuading by reward and chastisement and by the recognized distinction in law between culpable and inculpable ignorance. But this answer will hardly satisfy a sophisticated determinist. For one thing, we secure desirable results in the same way from animals and thus we may be the causes of our actions in no more original sense than they are of theirs. So when the objection is pursued that maybe the "appearance of good" (φαντασία) which motivated our early actions and dominated the whole later process of character formation was not in our own power but a matter of good or bad birth, Aristotle takes refuge in a simple *ad hominem* (telling, indeed, against the Socratic): if we are not to blame for our vices, neither are we to be credited for our virtues.[36]

Some have argued that Aristotle himself is in the final analysis a determinist. It seems unfair to force him into a position he would seem reluctant to take on a question he was unprepared to face (since he lacked the critical terms). It must be granted, however, that despite his quarrel with the Socratics, the only principles at his disposal, for all their value in explaining the psychology of action, leave him no escape.[37] This, as we have already pointed out, results from the absence of a concept of will—a faculty distinct from and superior to the sense appetite— and to the role ascribed in consequence to an undifferentiated ὄρεξις which gets the jump on reason in setting the goals of action before reason has had its own opportunity to judge them objectively. No distinctive human tendency corresponds to reason's own "natural light" [38] or to an "indifferent judgment" which is the condition for freedom. We can conclude this essay by remarking two consequences.

(1) It is noticeable that Aristotle's analysis of wrongdoing, whether this results from installed habit or from moral weakness short of it, is confined to the sort of action in which error in the practical judgment is caused by the sense appetite. There is no accounting for the so-called "spiritual sin." [39] This is an important omission. For although it is true that most character defect is traceable to this source (which is why temperance, though least in dignity, is the basic cardinal virtue) and that sins against temperance are "capital" in that they pave the way for all the others, the spiritual have their peculiar seriousness as suggested

by the various expressions used to describe them: they are wrongs committed *ex electione, ex industria, ex certa malitia* [40]— formulas which in their connotation of willfulness indicate that the trouble results, not from seduction by appetite, but from disorder in the will itself. This is a more serious kind of evil and harder to uproot. It is less difficult for the will to control a relatively alien sense appetite than to reverse its own inclination and deny its own chosen love. The more so since, in the typical case of pride, arrogance, jealousy, and envy, it is cherishing a genuine and superior value—one's real or fancied excellence—but without subordinating it to a higher.[41] An ethics which overlooks this special dynamism will be blind to a capital source of character deformation. It is no accident that the μεγαλόψυχος, Aristotle's "magnanimous" man, is such an unattractive fellow. Bad enough that he is too self-important ever to quicken his pace but, besides, he remembers only favors he has done, not those received. And he is displeased with reminders of them.[42]

(2) A second consequence: however responsible we may be for its formation, character once established not only disposes but necessitates and is itself inalterable.

> Once you have thrown the stone and let it go, you can no longer recall it, even though the power to throw it was yours for the initiative was within you. Similarly, since an unjust or a self-indulgent man initially had the possibility not to become unjust or self-indulgent, he has acquired those traits voluntarily; but once he has acquired them it is no longer possible for him not to be what he is.[43]

There is hope for the incontinent since his basic principle is that of right reason which is only momentarily obscured by the surge of passion. That is why he experiences remorse as soon as passion is satisfied. But for the self-indulgent the pleasurable good itself is the principle. And since he acts in full accord with it, he has no regrets and is in consequence incorrigible "for one who is without regret is incorrigible." [44] There is no hope of conversion for there is no sound principle—no equivalent of the axiom in geometry—on which to base a persuasive argument for reform.

There is so much substance to this perceptive diagnosis and it is so often confirmed by the facts of moral experience that it is all the more important that its limits be recognized. It has often been noted how on counts of both optimism and pessimism this understanding of man is opposed to that of Christian ethics. The latter with its special view of man's history and destiny has its properly theological grounds for affirming the universal need of grace for perseverance in good and the possibility of conversion, a basic "change of mind" or μετάνοια. Our present interest, however, is in the way the conception of will figures in the philosophical accounting for this difference.

Short of attaining its simply final good the will retains its essential indifference, and the goods which fall short of it include even the most exalted *bona honesta*. But this indifference implies a radical instability. And we have but to reflect on the concrete conditions in which moral life develops to appreciate what this means. Aristotle reminds us that virtue has no mean, but that "with respect to goodness" it itself is an extreme [45]—an *optimum potentiae*. Now, given the interdependence of the moral virtues and the requirement that to have any one of them perfectly we must have all the others—and perfectly; given the fact that a habit which involves the organism (through the sensibility) can weaken for want of occasions for its exercise;[46] given the role of temperament and the unlikelihood of a completely successful assimilation of it to reason, it can readily be seen that the opportunities for the subversion of prudence must always remain and in the course of nature alone will occasionally be realized. True, all things being equal—or not too unequal—character will prevail. Not because it has rigidly necessitated action, but because good actions are in accord with will's basic desire (its *volition voulante*) and with an acquired disposition which finds no obstacle opposing it. But could even the φρόνιμος himself—the man of genuine prudence—assure himself in advance of steadfastness in loyalty to any and all moral values under pressure of any and all solicitation? Would not this alone indicate a serious misjudgment about himself?

The same qualifications must be made vis-à-vis the evil character, although the situation here is much worsened since evil acts are not, as in the case of his counterpart, "out of character." There is much more to support Aristotle's pessimism than his optimism. For there is small likelihood of the great effort needed to overcome a dominant inclination whose strength results precisely from the will's frequent yielding in the past. In this sense we may indeed speak of a practical determinism. But if the will is not immovably fixed in adherence to the good, neither is it in evil, and so there remains even here the *possibility* of a way out (the technique of its actualization is another matter). For individual acts are individually willed whether in accord with character or not, and the will is not *necessitated* by the sense appetite or even by its own inclination. What is needed, of course, is a motive for a new kind of act which will go against the bias of character and make the breach through which successive acts can enter. *Hic opus, hic labor est.* For how are we to present as desirable what is in disaccord with one's already established values? It is for dynamic psychology to explore the ways for this dismantling of character. But, in general terms, we may say that, given the nature of the case, there will be some resort at the start to "medicinal" punishments (and rewards) to fight appetite with appetite [47] and restore the will's political power over it. This should provide the condition and the occasion for the gradual correction of vision itself, trusting here to the mind's native power of moral insight and the will's nature as rational appetency.

NOTES

1. An example of this type of ethical theory would be found in Erich Fromm's *Man for Himself* (New York: Rinehart, 1957).

2. An example of Stewart's determinism: "The individual is 'responsible' for acts which can be assigned to his *character* as immediate cause. His character is itself, as we now believe, the necessary product of the universe, and the circumstances which stimulate his character to put forth acts are likewise necessary products of the universe: but this does not relieve him of 'responsibility' and make his acts not 'free,' for 'free' applied to an act, means 'caused immediately by a character performing its functions in its environment.' Only 'the individual character in its environment' can put forth acts, and be 'responsible' for them—i.e., come in for their consequences" (*Notes on the Nicomachean Ethics*, 2 vols. [Oxford: Clarendon, 1892], I 227. See also his note at 1114B1).

3. See *Lysis* 219c.

4. *Nichomachean Ethics* (hereafter NE) 1.1094A20.

5. See René Gauthier and Jean Yves Jolif, *L'Éthique à Nicomaque*, 3 vols. Louvain: Publications Universitaires de Louvain, 1970, II 169–70 and the note at 1111B19 on βούλησις. See also D. J. Allan, *The Philosophy of Aristotle* (New York: Oxford University Press, 1970), pp. 53–54, 135; Sir David Ross, *Aristotle* (London: Methuen, 1966) pp. 199–200. For a differing view, see Jean

Ethics   41

Vanier, *Le Bonheur: Principe et fin de la morale aristotélicienne* (Paris: Desclée, 1965), pp. 159–60.

6. *De anima* III.10.433A13.

7. Ibid., II.3.414B.

8. Ibid., III.10. The argument is that man has a sense of the future and can distinguish a real from an apparent good.

9. *Sum. theol.* I, q. 19, a. 1 (for the existence of will in God) ; q. 80, a. 1. "Quia igitur est alterius generis apprehensum per intellectum et apprehensum per sensum consequens est quod appetitus intellectivus sit alia potentia a sensitivo" (q. 80, a. 2, c).

10. On the absence of this notion in Aristotle, see René Gauthier, *La Morale d'Aristote* (Paris: Presses Universitaires de France, 1958), pp. 86ff. Substantial portions of this work are translated in *Aristotle's Ethics*, edd. James J. Walsh and Henry L. Shapiro (Belmont, Calif.: Wadsworth, 1967), pp. 10–29.

11. NE I.13.

12. All that is required for freedom of choice is an advertence to a discrepancy between a particular good and the comprehensive good or *bonum in communi*. This need not necessarily require deliberation as a discursive process. The necessity of deliberation is owing to the potentiality of the human intellect and will and so is indicative of the imperfection of human freedom. As Yves Simon notes, this potentiality is rather an obstacle to freedom than its cause. See his *Freedom of Choice*, ed. Peter Wolff (New York: Fordham University Press, 1969), pp. 115–17.

13. It is here supposed that the dog is not a free agent—or if he is, so much the easier for our case and there will then be a canine ethics. We are pointing here to a difference in the way a dog "moves himself" to a bone in response to the stimulus of sense appetite—or even the way a man inspecting a menu indeliberately "decides" for fish over beef in unreflectively, and thus passively, following the suggestion of sense appetite and imagination—and the way that same man decides between accepting or rejecting a bribe. Here he must contribute considerations other than the good of money pure and simple and select those he will finally throw into the balance (*libra*, whence our term *deliberation*). True, the kind of motives really available to him and their weight, given his character and disposition, are of crucial importance. Of this, more later.

14. In this connection see the brief introductory chapter, "Images of Disorder," in Simon, *Freedom of Choice*, and pp. 115ff.

15. "The genuine man will not agree to recognize any foreign absolute. . . . Freedom is the source from which all significations and all values spring. It is the original condition of all justification of existence. The man who seeks to justify his life must want freedom itself absolutely and above everything else" (Simone de Beauvoir, *Ethics of Ambiguity*, trans. Bernard Frechtman [New York: Citadel, 1968], pp. 14, 24). The "serious" man, on the other hand, is one who would tolerate the regulation of his freedom by any absolute value which is not his own creation (see ibid., p. 46).

16. NE III.6.1139B4.

17. The analogy limps on two feet. Ship and steersman remain two "things," and the latter's activity does not "inform" the wheel.

18. NE VII.3.

19. Ibid., vi.2.1139A33. Aristotle's term is ἠθικῆς ἕξεως.

20. "What affirmation and negation are in the realm of thought, pursuit and avoidance are in the realm of appetite" (ibid., 1139A21). It should be remembered that speculative and practical intellect are the same faculty. The latter is but the extension of the former through the will. Practical intellect is founded upon speculative intellect—which is why the "truth" of moral action is ruled by the objective order which is the "measure" of speculative intellect. See Joseph Pieper, *Reality and the Good* (Chicago: Regnery, 1963).

21. NE i.13.1103A2.

22. Ibid., vii.3.1147B15.

23. Our point here is that the unconscious aping of the process of conscious motivation is indication that the latter is the normal one.

24. "Secundum vero naturam individui [virtus est homini naturalis] inquantum ex corporis dispositione aliqui sunt dispositi vel melius vel peius ad quasdam virtutes, prout scilicet vires quaedam sensitivae actus sunt quarundam partium corporis, ex quarandam dispositione adiuvantur vel impediuntur huiusmodi vires in suis actibus, et per consequens vires rationales, quibus huiusmodi sensitivae vires deserviunt. Et secundum hoc unus homo habet naturalem aptitudinem ad scientiam, alius ad fortitudinem, alius ad temperantiam. Et his modis tam virtutes intellectuales quam morales, secundum quandam aptitudinis incohationem, sunt in nobis a natura" (*Sum. theol.* i–ii, q. 63, a. 1, c). The final sentence of the article notes that one's capacity to feel compassion (*aptitudo ad miserendum*) stems from the corporeal disposition one has at birth.

25. See the concluding chapter of the *Ethics* where Aristotle prepares the transition to the *Politics* by a treatment of law as the instrument, in conjunction with the family, of moral education.

26. *Republic* 442c.

27. Ibid., 442A.

28. Plato's word. See his vivid description (ibid., 444B) of the disarray in the soul through the meddling of one part in the other's business.

29. NE vi.13. St. Thomas elaborates on this point both in his *In decem libros Ethicorum Aristotelis expositio* (Turin: Marietti, 1949), Lib. VI, lect. xi, and in *Sum. theol.* i–ii, q. 65, a. 1.

30. Shakespeare, *Hamlet*, I.iv.23–36.

31. NE vi.13. "Huiusmodi enim inclinatio, quanto est perfectior, tanto potest esse periculosior, nisi recta ratio adiungatur per quam fiat recta electio eorum quae conveniunt ad debitum finem; sicut equus currens, si sit caecus, tanto fortius impingit et laeditur, quanto fortius currit" (*Sum. theol.* i–ii, q. 58, a. 4, ad 3m).

32. Shakespeare, *Antony and Cleopatra*, III.ix.28–33.

33. See NE ii.4.1105A. Thomas comments: "Simul enim cum omnibus nutritur a pueritia ipsa delectatio, quia puer mox natus delectatur in lacte. Et ideo difficile est, quod homo possit subiugare hanc passionem, quae comparatur vitae, in hoc scilicet quod incepit cum homine a principio vitae. Et ideo circa delectationem maxime est virtus moralis" (*Expositio*, Lib. II, lect. iii, 276). See also *Republic* iv.429D which Aristotle may have had in mind.

34. See Thomas' *Expositio*, Lib. X, lectt. xiv–xv, as well as *Sum. theol.* i–ii, q. 95, a. 1, c.

35. *Laws* ii.653A–c (trans. A. E. Taylor, *Plato*, edd. Edith Hamilton and

Huntington Cairns [New York: Pantheon, 1966]). See also the fine passage in *Republic* III.401Bff. on preparing the child's tastes in advance "while still too young and unable to apprehend the reason (for the beautiful and the ugly)" so that "when reason came he would gladly welcome (the beautiful) as a friend, for by affinity he would recognize her."

36. NE III.5.

37. See Gauthier–Jolif, *L'Éthique à Nicomaque*, II 218–19, 576. Ross thus summarizes: "On the whole we must say that he shared the plain man's belief in free will but that he did not examine the problem very thoroughly, and did not express himself with perfect consistency" (*Aristotle*, p. 201). For the view of Aristotle as determinist, see, besides Stewart, Theodore Gomperz, *Greek Thinkers*, 4 vols. (London: Murray, 1964), Vol. IV, chap. 16.

38. While Aristotle recognizes a *jus naturale* or "just by nature" ($\phi v \sigma \iota \kappa \acute{o} v$) as distinct from the "just by convention" ($v o \mu \iota \kappa \acute{o} v$), it does not correspond (as Thomas apparently takes it to in his *Expositio* [Lib. V, lect. XII]; see Harry V. Jaffa, *Thomism and Aristotelianism* [Chicago: The University of Chicago Press, 1952], pp. 174–75) to a natural *law* or habit of first principles of practical reason by which we *naturally* discern good and evil and which *prescribes* and *forbids* accordingly. Such "natural-law ethics" was the work of theologians. It has been argued that for Aristotle even prudence itself ($\phi \rho \acute{o} v \eta \sigma \iota s$) discerns, not the goodness of the *ends* of action, but only the appropriate means to achieve ends already determined by the moral virtues, and that his ethical theory is in consequence basically empirical and not rational; the perception of good and evil originates in feeling and appetite, not in reason. In any case, since prudence is conditioned by right appetite, there will be for him *no* moral perception independent of it; we get our moral insights through early training in good habits. On the other hand, given a natural intellectual habit of first principles, or synderesis ($\sigma v v \tau \acute{\eta} \rho \eta \sigma \iota s$), *some* ineradicable recognition of good and evil will remain even in the vicious. On this whole question and its background, see Gauthier–Jolif, *L'Éthique à Nicomaque*, II 563ff. and J. Donald Monan, *Moral Knowledge and Its Methodology in Aristotle* (Oxford: Clarendon, 1968); more concisely in Allan, *Philosophy of Aristotle*, pp. 134–36.

39. *Sum. theol.* I–II, q. 72, a. 3. See q. 73, a. 5 for the question of their greater gravity in comparison with the "carnal."

40. Ibid., q. 78, a. 1.

41. *Sum. theol.* I, q. 63, a. 1, ad 4m and a. 2.

42. NE IV.3.

43. Ibid., III.5.1114A18 (trans. Martin Ostwald [Indianapolis: Bobbs-Merrill, 1962]).

44. Ibid., VI.7.1150A22.

45. Ibid., II.6.1107A8.

46. See *Sum. theol.* I–II, q. 53, a. 3.

47. NE X.9.1179B11. The point is developed by St. Thomas in his *Expositio*, Lib. X, lect. XIV, 2152: "Sed homo pravus, quia appetit delectationem, debet puniri per tristitiam seu dolorem, quemadmodum subiugale, idest sicut asinus ducitur flagellis. Et inde est, quod sicut dicunt, oportet tales tristitias adhibere quae maxime contrarientur amatis delectationibus; puta si aliquis inebriavit se, quod detur ei aqua ad bibendum."

3

Freedom and Morality from the Standpoint of Communication

ROBERT O. JOHANN

THE CONTENTION OF THIS PAPER is that much of the contemporary, and seemingly hopeless, confusion about ethical matters results from the fact that the standpoint from which they are investigated is inadequate to the task. In order to make this point, I shall, in the first part of what follows, take up the somewhat obscure notion of a *standpoint for reflection*. Besides a general sketch of its nature, this will involve distinguishing different possible standpoints a philosopher might adopt and indicating the relation between them. Here, I shall also spell out in general why it is important for a philosopher to adopt one standpoint in particular, that, namely, of communication, or what I shall call the dialogical standpoint. In the second part of the paper, the crucial bearing of this standpoint on any consideration of freedom and responsibility, and on the rational basis of moral action, will be developed in some detail.

STANDPOINTS FOR REFLECTION

The idea of a standpoint for reflection would seem to be borrowed from that of a standpoint for observation. It is, after all, a commonplace that what you can see at any particular time depends on where you are standing. What you will see from the mountain top will be different from what the villager in the valley can behold. The spatial location of the experiencer determines what can be given in his visual experience. In a similar way, where one stands emotionally, one's affective disposition, determines what one will find attractive or repulsive within the range of one's attention. And that range of attention itself is determined by the nature of one's preoccupation. A walk in the woods will be a different experience for a botanist and for a lover.

This all seems obvious enough and can perhaps be generalized in the following way. To speak of a standpoint is to speak of a disposition of an experiencing subject which in some way determines what is given in his experience. Such dispositions may be external (e.g., spatial) or internal (e.g., affective); they may be indeliberate and simply given (e.g., how we happen to feel) or they may be intentional and matters of self-disposition (e.g., the particular pursuit or activity we are engaged in). Thus we are accustomed to distinguish all sorts of standpoints from one another: the theoretical from the practical, the scientific from the aesthetic, the partial from the impartial, and, in the words of a recent television ad, that of the "business man" in each of us from that of the "human being." Moreover, we take it for granted that things look different when seen from different standpoints and that a large part of understanding what another person has to say consists of putting oneself in his shoes, adopting his standpoint.

So far so good. However a problem arises when the suggestion is made that different standpoints—and not all of them equally adequate—are possible in doing philosophy. Does not the philosophic enterprise define its own standpoint, which, quite naturally, is that of the philosopher (as distinct, say, from that of the scientist or the man of action)? In one sense, it clearly does. Indeed, that is the point we have just been making. To act intentionally is to orient oneself toward some goal, and this orientation will dispose the agent to attend to what is in accord with it, i.e., to matters which are relevant to realizing the goal, and to disregard what is irrelevant. The philosopher as such is engaged in a theoretical endeavor; he has turned aside from practical matters and the means to their accomplishment and is bent instead on a work of understanding and on what such understanding calls for.

And yet the question can arise: Must someone who is thinking do his thinking from the standpoint of one thinking? Must the philosopher philosophize from the standpoint of one doing philosophy? Granted: that one's spatial location defines the possibilities of one's visual experience, does that mean that, were one to seek to represent such experience, he would have to do so from where he is standing at the moment? Clearly, the answer to this last question is: no. Not only is it possible to represent here and now what was seen from some standpoint not currently occupied; it is also possible to represent how something would look from a standpoint in space which has never been actually occupied. Long before men landed on the moon it was possible to represent quite accurately how our earth would look from there. And the whole idea of the Copernican revolution depends on the possibility of "viewing" the solar system from a point other than where we are. A similar possibility would seem to obtain in the case of someone thinking. Granted: that someone thinking occupies a different standpoint and so experiences the world differently from someone otherwise engaged, it is not manifestly necessary that he think from the standpoint he currently occupies or in terms of the world as currently experienced. Occupying a standpoint and acting from that standpoint are not the same thing. To occupy a standpoint is to be disposed in a certain way and to have one's experience modified accordingly. But to act from a standpoint is to allow one's intentional life to be affected by the way that standpoint modifies one's experience. Thus, if someone is an interested party to a dispute, he will feel about the issues otherwise than if he were a neutral observer. But he need not, for that reason, act from the standpoint of an interested party. He may instead try to prescind from his feelings and to act from the standpoint of an impartial judge. So also a thinker as such is necessarily withdrawn from the other "in person" and is preoccupied instead with his ideas of the other. But he need not, on that account, think as if the other existed only in his ideas. Since he is thinking, he necessarily *occupies* the standpoint of the thinker. But nothing prevents him from thinking in terms of his experience, not as thinker, but as man of action.

That philosophers should do their thinking from this latter standpoint is the position for which John Macmurray has eloquently argued.[1] He claims that throughout its history philosophy has been developed instead from the standpoint of the thinker. Indeed, he contends that the present crisis of the personal is the result of the egocentrism and atheism which inevitably characterize a philosophy so developed when it is worked out to its logical conclusion.

Be that as it may—and I am inclined to agree with Macmurray in this regard—the point I want to make here is that there would seem to be three fundamental standpoints (not the *two* indicated by Macmurray) from which a philosopher can do his thinking. The first and perhaps the most natural—which is probably why it has been the dominant one in the history of philosophy—is indeed the standpoint occupied by the philosopher as philosopher. For one engaged in a work of thought, it would seem natural to proceed from the standpoint of thought, i.e., from the standpoint of one so engaged. What he will take as given and evident will be that, and only that, which is given and evident to the thinker in his very activity of thinking, viz., his own existence as thinker and the existence of his ideas or thoughts. Whether or not there exist anything beyond these thoughts to which they may be referred and by which they may be tested is problematic.

The second fundamental standpoint—also indicated by Macmurray—is that of the agent. To think from the standpoint of the agent is to do one's thinking in terms of what is disclosed, not to one thinking, but to one involved "hand to hand" with the other, to one as an agent of change. Since all action is "interaction" or, perhaps better, "transaction," an inclusive process involving the other along with the self as determinate existential factors, what is given and evident from this standpoint is precisely what was problematic from the preceding one, viz., the existence of the other. To think from the standpoint of action is to have the existence of the other just as evident and available to reflection as one's own. It is to have the other not merely as object of thought but as co-factor with oneself in an ongoing affair.

This is as far as Macmurray goes. But, as I have suggested, I do not think it is far enough. Indeed Macmurray's own work would seem to demand the addition of another dimension.[2] This further dimension is the third fundamental standpoint from which a philosopher can do his thinking, the standpoint, namely, of communication. For just as I am not merely a thinker but a factor in objective change (*idem ego cogito et ago*) and so can reflect in terms of my dealing with the other as well as in terms of my thoughts about it, so also I am more than an agent, I am a communicator. I am engaged with the other face to face as well as hand to hand. From this standpoint, the other exists for me, not merely as co-factor in an objective transaction, but as co-source of a dialogue. He is a partner with me in a shared experience. The newly evident here is being-as-subjectivity, being-as-I-and-you, being as transcending the realm of kind and as meaningful in its unique existence, its unique self-position. For the first time something is disclosed as significant, not only in terms of *what* it is or *what* it leads to, but precisely in terms of its being meant, its being something intended. Action is grasped, not merely as a modification of the other, but as a free response to the other's invitation. In communication, it becomes clear that reality is more than what is the case, more than the determinate and matter of fact; it is also, and more profoundly, the indeterminate and self-determining and what is a matter of intention.

Such, in very brief, are the three orientations which determine different ranges of what is given in one's experience and so provide different standpoints for reflection, different standpoints from which the thinker can do his thinking. It should be noted, however, that the relation between them is more intimate than has so far been expressly indicated. For the three intentional orientations we have described are not connected with one another on the sole basis that each of them can serve as a possible standpoint for thought. On the contrary, they are also related to one another as more or less inclusive orientations, as more or less inclusive standpoints.

What I mean is that each successive orientation involves the preceding one in addition to being distinctive in its own right. Thus agency involves thought while being more than thought, and communication involves agency while being more than agency. Man does not act as man except in terms of his ideas and judgments. Human action may indeed be defined as activity informed by thought. In like manner, one cannot communicate with another without effecting some change or modification in him. To be a communicator is also to be involved with the other as a co-factor in an objective transaction. But thought does not involve agency; nor does agency involve communication.

The first is thus exclusive of the second, and the second is exclusive of the third. To be engaged in thought is to be withdrawn from the other and wrapped up instead with one's ideas. Thought aims at modifying and improving, not the objective situation, but one's mental grasp of it. Likewise, to be engaged practically in the accomplishment of some task is to be concerned with the other as obstacle to be overcome or resource to be drawn upon, roles which the other has in terms of what it determinately is, not as a reality transcending the determinate. The outcome of an interactive process depends on the kinds of factors involved in it, not on whether their being that kind is something intended or not.

The relation between the three standpoints and the ranges of experience they determine is thus like that of three concentric circles with the innermost one representing thought or the theoretical, the outermost communication or the dialogical, and the middle one action or the practical. The dialogical standpoint is thus the most comprehensive one, and the theoretical standpoint the least comprehensive one, from which to do one's thinking. And this brings up the next point I want to discuss briefly, to wit, the importance for a philosopher of adopting the dialogical standpoint for his work.

The general importance of adopting the dialogical standpoint for philosophy is already suggested in our characterization of that standpoint as the most comprehensive. For, on the one hand, however variously the aim of philosophy has been interpreted, it is generally agreed that no dimension of experience lies beyond its scope. It seeks to understand, explain, account for, life or experience as a whole, to show how each of its multifarious dimensions is connected with all the others, to grasp it in its intelligible unity. On the other hand, the experiential data subject to the philosopher's organizing reflection will vary in range and scope depending on the standpoint from which he is doing his thinking. For, as I have explained, a determinate range of data corresponds to a determinate intentional orientation. Hence, whether or not the philosopher is conscious of the specific standpoint operative in his reflection, not to mention the possibility of adopting different ones, his very acceptance of something as given and something else as problematic is equivalently to adopt the corresponding orientation as his standpoint.

It is crucial, therefore, if his work is to be adequate to the full range of experience, that the thinker not restrict himself to building on what is disclosed in only some phase of his intentional life but avail himself of what is given in its comprehensive exercise. This comprehensive exercise of intentionality, however, is precisely his self-position as communicator, coparticipant in a common life. It is to be more than thinker, and more than shaper of the objective world. It is to be also and always in responsive relation with you. The standpoint of communication, then, or what we have called the dialogical standpoint, is that alone which is adequate to philosophy's goal. Only its adoption enables the philosopher to spend his time trying to understand the given in its wholeness rather than fruitlessly seeking to establish one or other part of it. What this means in connection with the problem indicated in the title of this paper, I shall now take up.

FREEDOM AND MORALITY

It is something more than an understatement to say that the idea of freedom is problematic for many of today's philosophers. It is problematic, not only as to whether or not there is such a thing, but also as to what it might possibly mean. One of the places where this comes out most often is in discussions of moral responsibility. The way the question is normally put has to do with the compatibility or incompatibility of accepting the principle of universal determinism and holding people responsible for their actions. And the way it is most commonly answered is to make some sort of assertion like the following: "A man's choice may be determined by his own belief, character, and desires (which, in turn, may be determined by previous causes), and yet be free and responsible."[3] In other words, being free and responsible for what one does and having one's choice to do it completely determined by antecedent causes are not viewed as mutually exclusive. On the contrary, holding for any "indeterminism" in human behavior is felt to make "things rather too 'chancy,'" as William K. Frankena puts it, and the idea of freedom as involving some kind of "self-determination" is regarded as "not yet . . . worked out in any satisfactory way."[4]

Now, the point of this section of my paper is to show how

views such as these, which I consider to be unhelpful, to say the least, are possible only when one is thinking from the standpoint of thought or from the standpoint of action. From the standpoint of communication, the basic meaning and existence of freedom, not only as a kind of self-determination, but as utterly incompatible with universal determinism, become part of the given. Let me explain how this is so.

The first step to be taken is to make a distinction between two ways of viewing any transaction. One way to look at it is as an external change or modification of a determinate situation or state of affairs. Things are otherwise than they were before the transaction or than they would be if it had not occurred. The other way to look at it is precisely in terms of whether or not it was *meant* or *intended*, and that on one side or both. Is the transaction which occurs also a deed, something informed by an intention, or is it merely an event, something which is not done but simply happens. The presence or absence of intentionality makes no difference to the way the transaction rearranges the determinate factors in the situation. It does, however, introduce a whole new level of significance. If you knock my hat on the ground, it may be an accident or it may be an act of aggression. The change in the external situation is identical either way; the hat which was on my head is now on the ground as the result of your movement. But whether or not you meant to knock my hat off can make a world of difference in our relationship. And this calls for closer examination.

What I am suggesting is that intentionality and the communicative or dialogical relationship go together. Apart from its having a bearing on relationship, being in the last analysis a "yes" or "no" to you, an acceptance of relationship or its rejection, the fact that an act is intentional or not makes no difference whatever. One is reminded of Kant's contention that the function of reason is to bring about a *good will*.[5] Were its ultimate purpose anything like man's happiness, well-being, or some other determinate state of affairs, this might more surely be accomplished by instinct. The self-justifying function of reason is rather the achievement of something beyond the empirically determinate, viz., a will which is good in its very willing. So also, analogously, here. The function of intentionality is not to bring about a specific rearrangement of energy systems. Its *raison d'être* lies beyond the whole order of empirical objects and the way such objects are arranged and rearranged. No arrangement of empirical objects requires intentionality for its accomplishment. What calls for and justifies an act as intentional is the achievement of a relation of subjects, of persons. Unless the sounds and movements you make are grasped as meant for me, they have no bearing, either positive or negative, on the reality of us. The moment they are grasped as meant, they do have such a bearing. But if there were no relationship, no "we" to be affected by your intentional activity, then your activity precisely as intentional would be utterly pointless and without meaning.

What this means is that if one is going to understand man's intentional life precisely as intentional, one will be able to do so only within the context of communication or, to put it in line with what has preceded, only if one thinks from the standpoint of communication. Since, moreover, his intentional life is man's life as a free and responsible individual, it is clear that freedom too is something which must be approached from the standpoint of the dialogical relationship if sense is to be made of it. For freedom is not "an unmotivated power of choice, . . . an arbitrary power to choose for no reason." [6] Neither does it imply that a person's activities are "chance events occurring in a haphazard or unpredictable manner." [7] Freedom is rather our capacity to communicate, to take a personal stand, to respond to meanings and not simply to react to stimuli, to participate in relationship.

Try to conceive a dialogue in which the "participants" are wholly submerged in a scheme of determinate and causal connections. Each is programed to react in certain ways to specific actions of the other which affect him. In such a state of affairs, neither "party" is more than a part of an overarching reality; neither is truly a self, a whole, something in himself and over against a genuine other. Each has import only in terms of *what* he is, the kind or class he exemplifies; neither has significance as uniquely existing, as a being transcending kinds. Can such a picture do justice to what you and I are aware of when we communicate with each other? Is not precisely what is lacking in it any dimension of meaning and intent? For to intend is more than simply to be aimed at some objective. Intending is a matter of aiming oneself. It implies a being, therefore, which exists in itself and not merely as a part of something else. Moreover, as an act of self-disposition, it presupposes a context in which such self-disposition is meaningful, a context, that is, within which a being active as a self has a place. Such a context, however, can be provided only by other selves, other beings capable of deliberate initiative and of responding to such initiative when invited to do so.

In other words, our experience of communication is our experience of an order transcending the empirically determinate and matter of fact, and so transcending purely causal sequence. It is an experience of intending and of being intended, an experience of entities who are active and significant, not as parts in a larger whole, but as wholes in themselves, as selves. It is, in short, our experience of freedom, of our capacity for personal relationship. To try to understand freedom apart from the communicative context—that is, to try to understand it in terms of man the thinker, or man the achiever—is to try to understand it apart from our experience of it. For thinking, even though it is an activity in which we may intentionally engage ourselves, does not derive its significance from being intentional, an act of self-disposition. Rather than being highlighted in thought, freedom and selfhood are effaced before the universal. So too when the standpoint is that of one who is aimed at bringing about an empirically determinate state of affairs. What is important here is the kind of actions taken, not their being intentionally taken. Small wonder, then, that from these standpoints freedom gets equated with something called choice, which itself is interpreted as an event in a causal sequence. If freedom is in fact our capacity to mean what we say and do, which in turn has import only in the context of personal relationship, then short of being approached from the standpoint of communication, it is bound to be misunderstood. For communication and relationship are precisely those realities for which intentionality and freedom are prerequisites, and to experience the former is to experience the latter.

I want to make some similar observations here in connection with ethical inquiry, and specifically with regard to two problems. The first has to do with the rational grounds for the choice to be moral, and the second (and related question) concerns the unconditional character of moral obligation. As in the preceding pages, I shall be arguing that thinking from the standpoint of communication provides a basis for resolving questions which otherwise remain insoluble.

It is not uncommonly held that, in the final analysis, the choice to be moral, to adopt the moral point of view instead of that of self-interest, is arbitrary. It is a function of, and manifests, the sort of person one happens to be. But it cannot be justified on any non-moral grounds. As one author puts it:

> Which way of life we choose just shows what kind of men we are. One cannot *condemn* the person who chooses egoism unless one takes the moral point of view and hence presupposes that the moral way of life is more justified than the egoistic way of life. The egoist could just as well condemn the moral person as a stupid fool, by taking the egoistic point of view and judging him to be foolish for not considering his own self-interest as the final standard for good and bad behavior.[8]

It is clear that such a position considers the moral interest as one interest alongside others, and just as the latter can get in one another's way, so the moral interest can get in the way of them all. In such a situation, a person has to decide just what his overriding values are going to be, and he must do so without there being anything on which to base his preference. One who makes moral values supreme equivalently adopts the moral point of view. It is, however, impossible to show that it is rational to do so.

This last contention, at least as it stands, is what I want to deny. It holds only from the standpoint of thought or the standpoint of action. The reason why it is impossible to justify the adoption of the moral point of view from the standpoint of thought is that, from that standpoint, it is impossible to justify the adoption of any point of view. For the adoption of a point of view is not only a specific action and so a determinate factor in an inclusive process of becoming, but also, and essentially, the act of a subject, a determinate way of being for an I, an act of self-position. This means that it is, not only something instrumental, but something final, something to be justified, not only in terms of what it leads to, but also, and especially, in terms of what it is. If, then, one point of view or, better, its adoption can be rationally preferred to another, it can only be because, as a way of being for the subject, it realizes an end or goal to which the

subject, precisely as a subject and prior to any acts of self-position, is ordered. In other words, what is needed is an end which
is not relative to the subject's intentions, but rather one to which
the subject's intentional life itself is relative. For only an end
which is antecedent to and transcendent of the subject's life as a
subject can be normative for it. For the standpoint of thought,
however, nothing is given which transcends the subject. What is
disclosed from that standpoint are simply the subject and his
ideas. Thus, from the standpoint of thought, whatever is other
than the subject is, even in its existence (since it exists only as
idea), relative to him. This being the case, not only is the subject's adoption of a point of view incapable of being justified;
from the standpoint of thought, no intentional act whatever can
be justified.

The same holds true for one thinking from the standpoint of
action. For, from this standpoint, both self and other appear as
variable factors in a process of change. In this light, the objective consequences of an act as specific—be that act the adoption
of a point of view or whatever—can be explored, but there is no
basis for its or their final evaluation. It all depends on what one
is looking for or happens to want. In other words, although the
standpoint of action discloses the other to exist independently
of the subject, it does not disclose it to have value independently
of the subject. The world disclosed here, no less than the world
disclosed from the standpoint of thought, is a world whose
values are relative to and dependent on the subject's intentional
life, not transcendent of it and normative for it.

All this is changed, however, when one thinks from the standpoint of communication. For from this, the dialogical standpoint, a world is disclosed for the first time to which the subject
in his very being and activity as a subject is relevant. It is the
world of the other as You, the world of transobjective relationship. Here is a world which not only transcends the subject but
is inclusive of him in his very subjectivity, a world within which
his intentions, not as factors in becoming, but precisely as ways of
being, making him one sort of person rather than another, are
finally meaningful. In other words, the dialogical standpoint
discloses a world which can ground the subject as subject. It is
one, therefore, to which the subject is ordered by nature and
prior to choice, the objective End of subjectivity, that to which

the subject himself is relative. It will be as a realization (or, respectively, a rejection) of this world, this End, that any intentional act, including the deliberate adoption of a point of view, achieves rational acceptability and justification (or deserves condemnation). Indeed, the adoption of the moral point of view is precisely the subject's commitment of himself to his objective End, that in responsive relation to which alone his life as a subject can be finally grounded. Far, then, from its being impossible to show that one acts rationally in adopting the moral point of view, it seems clear from the dialogical standpoint that adopting the moral point of view is the only fully rational course to take and that anything else is finally irrational. Let us put this analysis in a more schematic form.

To be a subject is to be able to choose one's course, to aim oneself at an end, to form intentions. One cannot choose (or form intentions) unless one has grounds for choice (for forming one intention rather than another). The ground of choice, in the last analysis, cannot be constituted such by any exercise of choice, but only by its own nature as ground and the nature of the subject as such, i.e., antecedent to choice. On the other hand, nothing can be the final ground for choice unless an exercise of choice is essential to its accomplishment. No observable state of affairs as such requires choice for its accomplishment. Only the transobjective relation of subjects (which, again, is disclosed only from the dialogical standpoint) requires choice for its accomplishment. The world of transobjective relationship, then, as that alone which can ground subjectivity (the capacity to choose), is the End to which being-as-subject is ordered by nature. It is, in Kant's sense, the objective end of man as subject and categorically claims his rational allegiance. Actions which are consistent with the pursuit of this end, i.e., actions which accord with the requirements of relationship, are morally right; those essential to relationship are obligatory; those inconsistent with relationship are morally wrong. By the same token, since only actions which are consistent with a subject's pursuing his objective end are finally rationally defensible, all immoral actions must be judged irrational and essentially self-frustrating. They are at one and the same time an exercise of choice and a negation of the ground of choice.

So much for the rationality of adopting the moral point of

view, and the relevance of thinking from the dialogical standpoint for an appreciation of that rationality. However, lest what
we have said be the occasion for new confusions, one final point
must be made, at least briefly. This has to do with the unconditional character of moral obligation. For when it is said that
only moral action is fully rational and that immorality is basically self-frustrating, at least part of the point being made is
that, for a rational being, acting morally is really in his own
interest and a fulfillment of his distinctive nature. In other
words, the alleged conflict between morality and self-interest is
actually a conflict between two levels of self-interest, between the
interest of the self as empirical object and the interest of the self
as rational subject. There is no question but that moral behavior
often runs counter to the interests of oneself as object. If what
has been said above is true, however, this same behavior is the
fulfillment of oneself as subject. The immoral person may gain
the whole world but he also "loses his soul." Whatever the cost
in empirical goods, the moral man at least "saves his soul." The
question arises, then: Does not this view make morality simply
a higher form of prudence? If it is simply a matter of self-
realization on one level rather than on another, a realization of
the self as subject in preference to the self as object, what happens to the unconditional character of moral obligation? Does
not the absoluteness of the moral claim rule out any reference to
self-fulfillment?

I think what this objection loses sight of is the essentially rela-
tional character of the self as subject which the dialogical standpoint discloses. One's nature as a subject is one's capacity for
transobjective relationship. To realize oneself as subject, therefore, is to put oneself in responsive relation with the Other-as-
You. It is to achieve a kind of fellowship which in principle is
universal. This means that the moral act, as a determinate
achievement of such relationship, is the embodiment of an all-
encompassing and final reality, something unconditioned and
absolute. It is, I suggest, the absoluteness of what is realized
through moral action which underlies the absoluteness of the
moral claim. It is because the subject finds himself ordered
through moral action to the achievement of a reality which is
all-inclusive that such action makes an unqualified claim on his
allegiance. In other words, reason is not morally normative for

the subject because it is his nature; on the contrary, his nature is morally normative because it is reason, i.e., a capacity for the all-encompassing and absolute.[9]

If, therefore, a person asks, "Why be moral?" the first and only real answer is that, since "being moral" is the realization of something absolute, it has an absolute claim on a person's rational allegiance. If, then, the question is pushed and one asks, "Why should I be interested in what has an absolute claim on my rational allegiance?" one has moved beyond the realm of rationality and so does not deserve an answer. Since, however, the motive underlying the question can be the fear that moral action may cost, it does not seem out of place to suggest that, in the last analysis, immoral action costs even more. Such a reason does not, of course, do justice to the absoluteness of the moral claim. But it may be a first step in reaching someone already committed solely to promoting himself. In short, to affirm that moral action is the only kind of action finally consistent with one's nature is not to affirm that the achievement of such consistency is the only rational basis, or even an adequate one, for being moral.

CONCLUSION

What was meant at the outset when I suggested that contemporary confusions about ethics stem from an inadequate standpoint should now be clear. Just as outside the context of action it is impossible to distinguish thinking from daydreaming or true judgments from false ones, so also outside the context of relationship it is impossible to distinguish the moral from the immoral, right actions from wrong. Just as action provides the context within which thought arises and in relation to which it is tested, so also relationship provides the context within which choice can arise and as promoting which alone it can be validated. The importance of the dialogical standpoint is that only from it can the unity of our intentional life be grasped. As John Macmurray observed (and all that precedes can be viewed as a commentary on his remark): "All meaningful knowledge is for the sake of action, and all meaningful action is for the sake of friendship." [10]

NOTES

1. See his *The Self as Agent* (London: Faber & Faber, 1957), especially the first three chapters.

2. Toward the end of his introduction to *The Self as Agent* (p. 15), Macmurray writes: "All meaningful knowledge is for the sake of action, and all meaningful action for the sake of friendship." This would suggest the three possible standpoints for reflection which I am advocating rather than the two (thought and action) which Macmurray explicitly develops.

3. William K. Frankena, *Ethics*, 2nd ed. (Englewood Cliffs: Prentice-Hall, 1973), p. 72.

4. Ibid., p. 76.

5. See the first chapter of the *Grundlegung zur Metaphysik der Sitten*.

6. John Dewey, *Theory of the Moral Life* (New York: Holt, Rinehart & Winston, 1960), p. 171.

7. See *Problems of Moral Philosophy*, ed. Paul W. Taylor (Encino: Dickenson, 1972), p. 280, where Professor Taylor contrasts these chance events with those occurring in an "orderly," scientific world.

8. Ibid., p. 495. This is part of Taylor's introduction to Kai Nielsen's "Why Should I be Moral?"

9. See Joseph de Finance, s.J., *Essai sur l'agir humain* (Rome: Presses de l'Université Grégorienne, 1962), p. 306.

10. See above, note 2.

4

Personal Freedom: The Dialectics of Self-Possession

Leonard C. Feldstein

In this essay, I analyze personal freedom in terms of two sets of triads which have dominated Western norms for human conduct: the scriptural ideal of faith, hope, and love, and the classical ideal of truth, goodness, and beauty. Pre-eminently the creature in search of freedom, man expresses that quest, I propose, as the stages, interpreted within a context set by these ideals, whereby he acquires self-possession. According to my thesis, first he *owns* himself primarily in relationship to himself alone; then he owns himself primarily as embedded within human society; finally, he owns himself more inclusively as enveloped by, yet participating in, the larger cosmos. Throughout this process, man progressively liberates himself. Therein, he reveals his essential being as an activity constituted by free, spontaneous creative acts, acts (nonetheless) witnessed, guided, and overseen, so I claim, by a personal presence. My purpose is to sketch, in terms of a correlation between the scriptural ideal and the classical ideal, the ground of human freedom, its inherent ambiguity, and the phases through which it is brought to fruition. In particular, I set forth the steps by which the self takes possession of itself as both condition and content of its evolving and ever-more-concrete freedom.

I

In Corinthians, it is written: "And now abideth faith, hope, love." Within this triad, hope includes yet transcends faith; love includes yet transcends faith and hope: for "the greatest of these is love" (1 Co 13:13). Sequentially, each virtue lays the ground whereby the remainder may be achieved. By the power of faith, the power of hope is activated. By the power of hope, the power of love is activated. According to my argument, the potentiation of faith, hope, and love is requisite for consummate freedom.

By "faith" I mean an entrusting. Trust,[1] I affirm, is the primordial quality of the acts by which the self orients itself toward its immanent possibilities for growth. Pre-cognizing the situation in which, from moment to moment, it finds itself, the self, in trust, acknowledges the options for action it therein discerns. In effect, it joins *its* (autochthonous) powers to powers resident within its situation. Thereby, the self becomes efficacious action.

Indeed, every present moment affords novel opportunities for action. By *present* moment I mean the moment in its *presence*, and "presence" in a double sense. On the one hand, I mean the haunting context in which the self apprehends itself with all its elemental powers—a context of factors not yet contoured which, entering into the composition of the self, potentiate those powers. On the other hand, I mean a gift, a present, whose donor, as yet unknown, is simply accepted. In both instances, this particular *instant*—fleeting, evanescent, fragile—is veritably a pre-*esse*. For it is the condition prior to *being*, i.e., being in the sense of an authentic *to be*—an enduring and, as such, a becoming. Moreover, by "presence" I mean that momentary being with another, however undefined and inarticulate, which, thus experienced as a gift, is at one and the same time a giving by a donor who though unknown is reassuring, and, reciprocally, a giving of the self to that donor. In this (first) stage along freedom's way, the bare, abstract potency of a process appears, a process whereby the self differentiates its options and primordially chooses or rejects those options. For, according to my usage, trust is the primordium of searching. Indeed, it *is* searching in its germinal state; it is that element primordially germane to searching. And searching, so I claim, lies at the heart of personal freedom.

This self-entrusting to the world implies that one initially orient oneself toward oneself unconsciously and merely immanently. As one passes, first, into a state of consciousness and, finally, into a state of self-consciousness, the simply reflex orienting elicited by the situation in which one is implicated is transformed into *reflective* orienting. Here, deliberation, hence deliberate attachment to a particular course of action, is evoked.

Indeed, deliberation, orientation, and attachment are related notions. For the conditions these notions suggest involve the element of balance or equilibrium. To be disoriented is to be in a state of imbalance. It is to be *de*-tached from those habitual attachments (to the presented gift) which constitute the primordial ground wherein one roots oneself—a ground destined to be progressively displaced from the circumstances, narrow and circumscribed, of early life toward a more inclusive and deeper ground. Moreover, the deliberation which accompanies this self-thrusting and the consequent quest for re-equilibration are correlative activities. Surely, "deliberation" and "equilibration" are cognate terms based upon the stem *librare*, so that "to deliberate" means *to weigh thoroughly* in the sense of *balancing* alternative possibilities.[2]

Accordingly, by the contingencies of life, one is constantly thrust into disorientation. Unforeseen constraints never cease to propel the person in one direction rather than another. Hence, as soon as detached, the self experiences its power for effecting reattachment; it is impelled to seek ever-new roots. Ultimately, security is found in the flux and ferment of the self's own powers —but only when those powers are experienced as joined to a "something" beyond the world. Here, no longer does attachment to particular objects prevail. Paradoxically, one has attained one's freedom by attaching oneself to an object so elusive as to be no object at all. In a kind of existential bewilderment, one secures oneself in that which itself is not secure: namely, in a self in process of continual formation and transformation, a self always in relationship to another which itself can be no object.[3]

For, always, one must find one's way about the world as though one were in a labyrinth. Yet, one's explorations inexorably lead one back to one's self. Indeed, in the final analysis, this labyrinth *is* the self, a self which ever strives to *own* itself amid the kaleidoscopic fluctuations of the world. Accordingly, faith consists in a spontaneous un–self-conscious rootedness in a relationship between the self and the immanently enveloping process which is the world experienced, as faith brings itself to fruition, as only initially stable and dependable; for, on deeper inspection, I stress, the world reveals itself as inexorably in ferment. Hence, trust eventuates (so I shall argue) in reliance upon an inclusive personal witness,[4] a witness both immanent within one's own self-development and transcendent to it—a personal witness to one's own being and growth. As the self thereby roots itself in itself, and as thus experienced as ultimately witnessed, it is clarified and made more substantial. Each present moment is felt as, in effect, a concrete particular: stable and solid, yet but an occasion of experience ever in process of metamorphosis, efflorescing by reflective elaboration into a new occasion.

However, once achieved, the freedom of trust cannot rest content with a mere string of presents: each *sui generis*; each an enveloping presence; each, in effect, a witness benign, should trust reign, but, if distrust supervenes, malignant.[5] For freedom is a perpetual stirring, an insatiable restlessness of the self. To be, freedom must transcend its own mere floating in a particular moment. It must constitute the *duration* of a present, a present which flows toward and into a future. It must pass from the phase of trust to the phase of hope. For hope concerns the continuity, and not a mere contiguity, of present moments. By implying a future, a durable solidarity of moments also implies a past—a past which expresses the present as the latter perishes into a new present which is the future about to be. Indeed, to hope is to secure oneself in a destiny which is an ineluctable outgrowth of the immediacy of the moment. In hope, the self risks, from moment to moment, its integrity, its wholeness, its balance; it dares thus to risk in hope that a solidarity of moments will thereby emerge. For hope concerns survival, survival despite unfortuitous contingencies.

Accordingly, the ground for survival, so hope affirms, *is* this solidarity of past with present, this passage of what had been present into what will be present. In hope, an Imago of all that had been is etched upon every present which appears. A novel scheme of values, a new priority of intensities, is assigned this Imago. A unique pattern of contrasts is shaped. In addition, hope affirms the solidarity of present with future. It discerns the lineaments of sheer possibility; it foresees the transmutation of mere potency to actuality; it oversees the activity of selection and rejection, the activity whereby these possibilities are contoured into ever-new configurations of actuality. Finally, thus affirming the pregnancy of the present with the seeds of the past as they blossom toward the new creations of the future, hope affirms its own continuance. For hope catalyzes the renewal of hope. Its continuity is grounded in the continuity of time itself—time *in concreto*, time rich with the lesser durations which flow to ever-more-inclusive durations.[6]

Once faith and hope are established as the prevailing conditions of human existence, the way is opened by which human freedom may receive its veridical ground. For freedom requires, first, that one fully entrust oneself to the fleeting moment, in faith, that one give oneself up to the objectively *spatialized* sphere of encounter; and freedom further requires that one entrust oneself to every duration, in hope, that one give oneself up to the subjectively *temporalized* sphere of self-encounter. Indeed, only this conquest of time itself by hope, and the consequent rooting of oneself within the temporal process, will allow the consummately *material* self to emerge, a self actively in relationship with the world likewise experienced as substantial. Surely, thus to bring one's personhood to fruition in this experience of freedom, the self must articulate the space of its existence; only thereby may it feel the freedom to expand its own powers vis-à-vis the world. Further, it must enter into durable relationship with the objects it discriminates within this space; only thus may it feel the expanding powers of the world in relationship to itself.

For space is engendered in the wake of the flow of time; as time temporalizes itself, it correlatively leaves spatial depositions. These depositions spread out as successive sets of moments, one set stratified upon the other and, as spatial, similar to eternally present moments. Indeed, from this point of view, space is the insinuation of eternity into time. Beyond that, it is that arresting of time which is no mere evanescent point, but a solidarity of objects. For space is a field of relationships among these objects, objects co-ordinated as a context of action. As such, space is the "region" toward which objects, construed as processes, strain for interconnection. It is the virtuality of full relatedness. Conversely, time is the flowing of spatial arrangements into one another. Ultimately, time is the virtual movement into futurity which inheres within every spatial increment. It is the becomingness of space. Accordingly, amid the eternal spread of all consummated present moments, time is the inexorable process character of reality. Hence, at bottom, the solidarity of objects is a flowing forth, a "concresence"[7] of those objects: a bringing to birth of their latent possibilities as real, concrete entities. The former expressing hope and the latter expressing trust, process and eternity are, appropriately construed, ingredients of love.

Under this perspective, human freedom consists, in the last analysis, in the self giving itself to a matrix of progressively crystallizing relationships. Within this process, the self finds itself; it experiences compresence, a sense of dwelling momentarily with the eternal. Herein it discovers its own ground and distinguishing traits; it acquires the capacity to receive into its constitution the gift of the variegated *relata* to which it thus (spatially) relates itself; it is liberated to feel its way into the very texture of those *relata* so that, conversely, it might, when *they* will have received a sufficient degree of sentiency, accept the reciprocal apprehending of itself *by* the *relata*. In short, freedom is the activity by which the self attains to possession of itself in relation to that which, though wholly other than it, is nonetheless profoundly attuned to it. For, at bottom, freedom is the mutual attunement of self and other. In freedom, the rhythms of each enmesh with each. Renouncing itself as merely self-enclosed, the self ceaselessly affirms as the ground whereby it individuates itself its participation within a context of relations—relations which, in their consummate shape, are relations of love. Hence, faith and hope ground the possibility for the emergence of love; love is the condition requisite for the emergence of freedom from its merely germinal state.

When I speak of the self-possessed man, I mean a man in possession of his faculties: his gifts and his sensibilities. Thus truly owning one's own resources, one is free so to orient oneself toward the contingencies of life that one can only enrich the quality of that life. For, no matter how constrained by the obstacles which inexorably intrude themselves from every direction, the self is empowered to dwell in vibrant peace with itself. Moreover, so dwelling, it experiences itself as likewise dwelling within, hence empowered radically to accept, a relationship between itself and a witness to its actions—ultimately, an inclusive, enveloping presence at first dimly though always hauntingly perceived, then discerned with increasing clarity. In an attitude of ever-more-profound acquiescence, without, however, ceasing to affirm its own essential autonomy, the self dwells, as it were, in the interstices between itself and another; by stages, it detaches itself from bondage to the other, while, correlatively, it gradually attunes itself to that other; and, in the last analysis, it attaches itself only to the source whence springs all relationship. In effect, the free self—or, more accurately expressed, the self in process of freeing itself—acquires an attitude of sensitive respect for the contingencies of existence, including the contingency of its very self.[8]

In consequence, the obstacles one confronts, and unremittingly must orient oneself toward, present themselves in stratified fashion, each set layered upon an antecedent set and interacting with that set; a progressive detachment from that to which one had hitherto been attached; a grieving over the loss of an ineluctably perishing past; a detachment which thrusts one again and again into the solitude of one's own evanescing *I*—yet, the solitude, I repeat, of the relatedness of presences which transcend the finite; the infinitude of an enveloping personal witness incarnate, not in a particular object, but in the constant flowing forth of endless successions of matrices of objects.

A holy triad: faith, hope, and love! The crown of faith is hope; the crown of hope is love. Having already declared that without love there is no freedom and that the inmost and most elemental ingredient of freedom *is* love, I may now affirm: love unfolds in a procession of stages, the stages whereby the obstacles to which I have referred are, one by one, not so much conquered as acquiesced to; love presupposes resignation; love entails tranquillity; love proceeds at times calmly, at times ecstatically, but, however it unfolds, love always aims at vibrant peace.

II

To facilitate my quest for the meaning of personal freedom, I now note certain etymologic surprises.[9] In its usual sense, *free* is derived from the Old English *fri*, meaning "not in bondage or constraint." In this usage, freedom is defined by negation. It is not *freedom toward* such and such an orientation, but *freedom from* such and such constrictions. However, when further pursued, "freedom" may be traced to the Old High German word *fridu*, which means *peace*—the original of the modern German *die Friede*. Moreover, in Flamboyant German, from the time of

Walther von der Vogelweide, *freien* signifies "to marry." In turn, the latter may be traced to Old High German *frijon,* which means "to love," and this term is, in its origin, grounded in the Sanskirt *priyate,* meaning "he loves." Indeed, "to marry" surely implies a bond, but not, in its origins, a bond*age.* On the contrary, it implies a union, an attunement of lovers, a completion of each in the other. Hence, involved in the very roots of our contemporary word "freedom" are the ideas of both *peace* and *love* (the latter in its reciprocal sense). Surely, moreover, the concept, though not the word, "peace" is related to the intertwined concepts of *faith,* or trust, and hope. To be at peace with oneself requires that one be both trusting and hopeful—in the senses previously mentioned. And both trust and hope, I repeat, ground and condition the possibility for love.

Continuing this etymologic exercise, I note the origins of the word "person" in the Greek πρός and ὄπα (from ὄψ [or ὦπα from ὤψ]). In classical Greek theater, the word refers to a mask placed before the eyes and the face in order to dramatize certain qualities which the actor symbolizes and, in addition, to communicate this symbol to the audience. Moreover, ὄπα is related to such words as "sonorous"; i.e., the effect of this mask was to amplify the voice, to draw forth speech in powerful resonances. Thus resounding as a vocal aura which emanates from the actor, and radiates toward his audience, the spoken word envelops the audience in the charisma of the special qualities intended to be transmitted. Indeed, to speak forth with resonance is to declare some profound inner condition, a state of the psyche which resides deep within the person. Moreover, it is to communicate the intentions, the depth, and the scope of the inwardness of the actor, the labyrinthine character of his psyche. Finally, it is to affirm through the inflections, the sonorities, of the words he utters his essential and inmost being.

Combining the terms "personal" and "freedom," I now take certain liberties within my etymologic exploration. I affirm as to the meaning of these linked ideas *a passing out of a (passive) stage of bondage (i.e., the contingencies) through love grounded in faith and hope, and the bonds of love, to an (active) state of peace.* In this passage, the one who dwells *through* bondage toward love and, ultimately, toward peace, declares, in his speechifying, his authentic inwardness. In effect, within the depths of one's being one discovers the words by which one might express, and comportmentally constitute, oneself a living exemplar of the questing man. Accordingly, "to be free" means to be in a state of personal harmony and authenticity that one might transcend all bondage, and dwell in peace and in love. This dwelling is a double dwelling: a dwelling with oneself and a dwelling with another, whether the latter is thing, organism, or person; and each mode of dwelling exhibits its own phases and characteristics.

What is the nature of this dwelling in both its active and its quiescent aspects? In recent years, *to be free* is associated with a power to do and to change. However, the earlier meaning proposed in my etymologic excursion implies an acquiescence and a resignation, a giving of oneself up to whatever will induce harmony among the diverse parts of one's being as it stands in relationship to another. More comprehensively: to be free is to engage in a dialectical interplay between the active and the quiescent—and this with respect to the constraints of human existence, constraints imposed both from within and from without. Accordingly, freedom concerns the issue of how one is to orient oneself toward those constraints which limit the possibilities for (free) action. These questions arise: Does one seek to alter constraint? Does one alter oneself in reciprocal co-adaptation with constraints as they are altered? Does one alter oneself exclusively? Pressing back limits involves prior acceptance of limits. For the limits to human existence do not essentially recede by force. On the contrary. They recede only consequent upon their acknowledgment and their understanding, their acceptance in resignation and tranquillity. From this point of view, to search is so to search among limits that one will discern their import for, and impact upon, one's personal existence.

What is the essential element of this searching wherein freedom consists? I affirm: personal freedom is not a *given* state of human existence; it *is* human existence. For existence is ἔκστασις, the self standing forth and declaring itself, standing forth rooted in its own powers for relating both to itself and to what is other than itself. Thus standing forth, the self takes hold of successive options, organizing its choices into patterns which, seen retrospectively, are foci in the searching activity—an activity unfolding within perspectives which become ever more inclusive. In this process, the self *exists* in the sense that it *freely* exercises restraint and power.

Again, I ask, wherein consists human freedom? So often it is claimed that freedom is an illusion nursed by man to designate his ignorance concerning regions of determination concealed from awareness. Alternatively, freedom is regarded as a myth cultivated to hide despair over one's radically contingent status in the universe. In my account, I treat freedom as neither illusion nor myth, but as an essential constituent of man himself, *the* ontologically essential element of his being. But freedom is not a mere state of openness with respect to options for action which may severally be entertained as indifferently capable of realization. Quite the contrary. For I regard freedom as sheer reflexivity. It consists in every man's addressing himself—whether this addressing is articulated or not, or whether it is spoken in words or felt in silence, and whether awareness of this self-addressing is explicit or immanent, conscious or unconscious. In effect, in thus addressing himself, every person *is* a *reflexive* process of freeing *himself*. The idea may be better rendered in German: *ich befreie mich*. For I am constantly in the act of making myself free. Not free from bondage; not free merely to choose; not free only to exercise power. But beyond these modalities of freedom—free to undertake a journey, to engage in a passage, a transition, through a succession of attachments each of which, however, ineluctably falls away, *from* imbalance and disorientation *to* harmony and re-orientation. Not only harmony of self with self, but a harmonizing of self in relation to a something outside of self. Not, however, a something which is, strictly speaking, a thing. For to free oneself is so to orient the self, amid its disorientations, that it roots itself in its very self; and, being reflexively constituted, the self is surely *no* thing.

Accordingly, if I inspect, one by one, the inner fabrics of my being, revealing my moods, my fantasies, my dreams, my sensations, I find that contingency reigns as inexorably within me as the resistance I meet when I traverse the world about me. I find myself constrained both from within and from without. I am adrift in a sea of emotions quite as ineluctably as I am adrift in a sea of motions. For motions proceed from without, and therein terminate. Emotions proceed from within, impinging on the outer. Where may I find anchorage? No longer in any mood, image, or external object. I find my roots, my only roots, within the very *I* which is in quest of those roots. I secure myself in the very act by which I search for my security. But this succession of acts is a ferment which itself has no anchorage. It is elusive, transitory, evanescent. And so I am step by step led to root my searching activity itself in a "something" which lies beyond that activity. Yet this "something" cannot be, ultimately, my own self. It surely cannot be the world about me. For both are in flux and upheaval; both are in perpetual transit. My searchings are always enveloped by a beyond beyond those searchings. They are haunted, embraced, and tendered by that beyond. It can be no material beyond. Quite the contrary. It is a beyond which is personal. Yet, no person. It is a beyond which is ultimately mine, and yet it is not me. Yet it is a beyond which is experienced as in concernful relation to me.

Accordingly, to be free is to search both within oneself and without; it is to anchor oneself, in one's searching, in a relationship between oneself and an all-enveloping personal witness to that searching; it is to give oneself up to the search that this witness be a living presence, a presence which both transcends the self and is immanent within it; it is to give oneself up in faith, in hope, and in love. For in faith, one discovers one's self: its possibilities, the constraints imposed upon it, the truth regarding those constraints. In hope, one discovers another counterposed to the self: *its* powers, the types of interconnection between the two, the good as residing within the values it places upon that other. In love, one discovers the relationship between self and other, the reciprocation between the two: *their* modes of co-adaptation, the rhythms of interpenetration and autonomy, the beautiful as constituting successively higher ways by which they are harmonized.

Accordingly, I find a correlation of import for my concept of freedom, a correlation between the scriptural triad, faith, hope, and love, and the classical triad, the true, the good, and the beautiful. To explicate the nature of this triad, its internal nuances and intricacies, is to reveal the deeper meaning of personal freedom. To anticipate: faith allows one to reason, that he attain truth; hope to act, that he attain goodness; love to create, that he attain beauty. For, within the limits prescribed by faith, once the quality of these limits is apprehended, man reasons; within the limits prescribed by hope, once the resistance afforded by these limits is sensed, man acts; within the limits prescribed by love, once a relationship to these limits is established, man creates. Thus, I correlate three pentads: faith, reason, truth, quality, and personal space; hope, action, goodness, resistance, and personal time; love, creation, beauty, relationship, and personal "matter" or substance. Freedom is the quest of man to probe, in a multitude of concrete ways, the inner meaning of this correlation.

III

In general, to be free, so I have argued, is to be aware of oneself as actively orienting oneself toward oneself in relation to an object. It is being with the other as self-consciously oneself, therefore self-affirming one's own being. In a word, freedom consists of owning oneself in the context of a significant relationship. According to my proposal, this state of existence reveals itself in three unfolding modes: from the side of subjectivity, these modes are faith, hope, and love. Their import has already been set forth. From the side of objectivity, I have yet to argue, these modes are truth, goodness, and beauty. In my account, to be free is to search in peace, along the way of faith and hope, that love be achieved.

To this end, one apprehends, in freedom, one's subjectivity as ever-changing, ever-deepening in relation to an object which, likewise, one experiences as ever-changing, ever-deepening. An increasingly differentiated subjectivity is perceived as such only in correlation with an increasingly differentiated objectivity. For, I now stress, self and world cannot be dissociated. Accordingly, freedom is a self-progressive activity, an activity which unfolds in stages, and thereby gradually discloses and articulates its latent content. Within these stages, the inner connections and the mutual dependencies of self and other are apprehended. Now, claiming that the stages of freedom are the phases of truth, goodness, and beauty, I wish to amplify my account of these phases.[10]

Initially, I have already suggested, one gives oneself in faith to an object which is as yet no veridical object but which, in fact, is a mere datum—a datum, however, for which no donor is yet specified, hence an object which as such is fleeting and evanescent. Within limits accepted as prescribed, one speculates freely—in effect, exploring and specifying those limits. In a word, one gives oneself up to the present, but to a present not yet construed as *presented*, i.e., as a present or a gift. Simply: one allows the object to present itself in its immediacy as a kind of abstract universal. Hence, thought journeys among these immediacies, striving to give them a form and systematically rendering that form by lawful connections. At this stage, freedom, earlier equated on its subjective side with faith, is the endeavor to conceptualize the truth: not truth in its ultimate shape, but truth merely as a pattern of invariant connections. Hypostasizing the immediacies of the present, symbolic forms are created which, beginning with common sense, culminate in science. The inquirer secures himself in these forms, received as necessary and determined, without yet penetrating to the action which engenders the data thus cogently organized. For, in this stage, the contours of consciousness are mapped. In its uttermost scope, the spatiality of the activity of "conscious*ing*" is engendered. Inquiry frames this activity as an assemblage of assertive judgments, systematically co-ordinated, regarding a presumptively objective realm.

Accordingly, by truth, I mean the allowing of one's mood, volitions, and thoughts to be determined essentially by an object to which, that this end be achieved, one actively gives oneself up. Dwelling within the context of a truthful orientation toward oneself in relation to that object, one allows oneself to be enveloped by it. Indeed, the quester after truth is so pervaded by the object that, in effect, it prescribes the contents, the order, and the shifting directions of his reveries, converting them to the fixity of a determinate rational structure.

In this phase, no distinction is yet made between things, organisms, and persons. In effect, these classes of entities are assimilated to one another. Only superficial differences among them are affirmed. Hence, each sphere is conceived as an ordered manifold of objective relationships, even though the inquirer acknowledges that the mode of being by which the emerging self *relates* to a given sphere is peculiar to the special, objective character of that sphere—granting, however, that such modes are not yet, on this level, clearly articulated. Moreover, these spheres—namely, the realms of things, organisms, and persons—themselves are construed, in the phase of truth, to be interconnected as constituting a single, objective manifold. For truth rests upon the faith, elemental and irreducible, that the world is a *reliable* presence; the inner connections between one manifestation of that presence and another are not yet affirmed. Accordingly, Hume's analysis of causality is appropriate for specifying the peculiar features of this phase. Only, as he argues, habit grounded in custom may validly be proposed as holding together, as it were, the as yet intrinsically dissociated moments in the appearance of reality. Indeed, reality cannot yet be acknowledged as the subsistent ground for the succession of appearances. Nevertheless, one does not desist from seeking the specific manifold which is *truly* pointed toward by the object; reveries come and go, and among them one finds that true manifold—i.e., that manifold which, in conformity with the object one possesses, discloses the form of that object.

So as soon as the inquirer yields himself to this objective order of events, postulating rational connections between conceptual representations of them, he becomes aware that he is truly re-*presenting* what had already been experienced as, however fleeting, ineluctable presences. Hence, the object is, so to speak, suffused by his representations of it. Thereby, it is experienced as solid and durable. But since the object is now, as it were, rationalized, i.e., infused with the subjectivity of the inquirer, it is by virtue of its newly perceived durability also conceived as, equally, malleable. For, insofar as it is thus imbued with subjectivity, that object is alterable. Imagination projects itself upon the object to invest it with new qualities. Moreover, within the limits prescribed by its possibilities for resisting, the object *qua* object is also alterable. Its sheer physicality proscribes numberless imaginational possibilities. Hence, the object is discerned as doubly changeable. For *qua* objective, it is capable of undergoing physical manipulation; and *qua* subjective, it is the project of human discrimination. In effect, a kind of dialectic unfolds between what the object is in and for itself and what that object is for another. Each status presupposes, requires, and conditions the other. Never is the object perceived in independence of these intertwinings of objective and subjective elements. At one and the same time, it is a projection of the self *and* self-sufficient as enduring in radical independence of the self. Because of this double status it is indeed changeable, and often dramatically so. Accordingly, freedom now passes into its next phase, a phase in which the self actively orients itself toward the object which it experiences as alterable through the intricate manipulations it is capable of undergoing.

In effect, one gives oneself up in hope to the present, actively taking hold of the fleeting moment. In this context, the present reveals itself to be a solidarity of presents, a duration. The object is grasped as an unfolding. There is expectation and anticipation, hence, futurity. Temporality and, indeed, historicity arise. Correlatively, the object is now accepted as itself the product of activity even though activity is as yet but bare activity. The succession of present moments is experienced as, at bottom, an integrality of those moments; and the latter, in effect, the objectivity of the object, is revealed as its resistance—hence the donation of a donor, the conception of whose particularity and concreteness is adumbrated but not yet probed in its hidden depths. Nevertheless, this durational flow is apprehended as also created by thought, which conceives itself to have welded the immediacy of present moments to a temporal solidarity. In experiencing the object as a sharply contoured duration etched against a non-articulated background, one perceives the limits of that object as tangible, therefore alterable. Thought grasps itself as empowered to press beyond those limits. No longer content merely to search into them, it allows itself not simply to be affected by the limits in reflex fashion. For thought itself sets in motion events which effectively change those limits.

Accordingly, thought is capable of apprehending itself as shaping, not only an idea of limits to which it must conform, but, in addition, an ideal regarding what those limits *ought* to be. Hence, thought becomes incarnate in action. No longer is it satisfied with merely making assertions or declarative judgments. On the contrary. It embodies itself in its very acts to constitute active judgments, judgments which *change* the object. In hope, therefore, thought grasps itself, probing its own inner depths which lie beneath the surface of its awareness; and, in its probing, it does not merely reveal a manifold of immediate presents. For, beyond conceptualizing that manifold, thought so

relates itself to the object that it reshapes the object in accordance with an ideal drawn forth from those inner depths. In this
process, thought grasps that relationship as involving, as essential elements, resistance, action, reaction. In turn, these constitute
a *temporal* manifold, durational time which engenders in its
wake specific spatial assemblages of merely present moments.

Gathering together data initially apprehended as evanescing
spatiality, lawful though the latter be, thought now conceives
consciousness as itself surrounded by unconscious depths, depths
not yet revealed regarding their specific content and possibilities, but depths which counterpose as yet unexplicated ingredients to the ideal which thought has posed for itself. Hence,
thought now first perceives a conflict to reside within its own
self-consciousness regarding the objects it durationally constitutes. Still, insofar as thought poses an ideal and, accordingly,
endeavors to transform objects for the purpose of bringing them
into conformity with that ideal, it now exhibits itself as intrinsically purposeful and, as such, directive of such changes in the
object as will refashion the latter into something good.

In the relationship which is truth, I have argued, the object
is authentically objective. For, thrusting itself against the subjectivity of the self, it counterposes itself to the latter as intrinsically unalterable. Encountering the resistances offered by the
object, the self must come to terms with it by forming, in the
long run, (assertive) judgments about it. On the other hand, in
the relationship which is the good, I now propose, the object
through its very conception has been converted to a subject, a
subject to which the self applies itself to the end that the former
bend itself to the will of the latter. For it is the subject of alteration. Now, the self has been transformed to an irresistible objective force, a set of durable intentions to which the object transformed to subject by the very actions of the self must bring
itself into conformity. In effect, the roles of subject and object
have been interchanged. No longer construed as evanescent phenomena which may only be stabilized through their representation as laws, the world is experienced as durable material which
may be molded in accordance with principles prescribed by
what is now interpreted as the lawful fabric of the self. For the
latter in effect announces to the world the manipulative possibilities resident within it—always, of course, limited by what

hitherto had been prescribed by the world to the self as the truth of the latter for the former. The domain of the merely cognitive has passed over into the domain of the veridically ethical.

For the truth of the world for the self is but one ingredient within a larger perspective upon the relationship between world and self, a perspective which may only be designated the *goodness* of the world for the self and, by extension, for the community of selves. Indeed, when the object is construed as durable, hence alterable, material, it presents itself to the self as a scheme of possibilities for transformation in those ways which are deemed by the self as beneficial for it, thus gratifying its needs. In the first instance—namely, truth—the self orients itself toward the world in such a way that, thus entrusting itself, it gives itself up to that world. But, in the second case, that orientation (essentially one which rests upon faith in the continuance of the world, despite alterations the world may undergo by the very actions of the self) involves the object's yielding itself to the self as a matrix for such potential alteration. In addition, the relationship between trust and truth presupposes an immanent, germinating faith and, correlatively, goodness. For, ultimately, the stability of the world—in effect, the uniformity of nature— entails the consequent construal of the world as potentially alterable in accordance with the intentions of the self. Indeed, this assumption grounds the very possibility of truth. But this ground becomes explicit only when the phase of truth has been consummated. Only then may the second phase, goodness, be liberated as the conscious objective of the self to achieve *its* consummation.

A dialectical unfolding is posed. Within this process, the self achieves its freedom by stages. Initially, a passive self is counterposed to a dynamic object. In truth, the self relates to itself as essentially passive in its relation to an active world. To gain this experience, the inquirer must perceive the object from many points of view, illuminating it under variegated perspectives, that subsequently he may conceptually integrate these diverse facets. Yet the very acts by which integration is attained lead to his re-interpreting that object as part of a real continuum, an objective order of nature. Placed in various positions that it may reveal itself as woven of rearrangeable objective elements, factors within bare undifferentiated fact, the object itself discloses the specific ways in which the self might maneuver with it. Correlatively, the spontaneity of the self as it strives to effect change is revealed. Accordingly, the determinate character of nature imputed to it by cognitive judgments framed by the self exhibits itself as presupposing an inquiring person, a self which experiments and, as it experiments, incidentally gratifies or frustrates its own desires. But the very efforts thus to gratify reveal the insatiability of the self; and this disclosure—namely, that the self is vacuously infinite in its desires for remolding the world— unveils a double terror: that of the abyss of the world, in its malleability; that of the abyss of the self, in its vacuity. Lurking in the phase of the good, this terror replaces the terror residing in the phase of truth: namely, that of the rigidity of the world vis-à-vis the impoverishment of the self.

Now, the self dynamically relates to itself as it dynamically relates to a *passive* world. An insignificant self vis-à-vis the world, wherein the world is conceived as threatening to annihilate the self, gives way to an insignificant world vis-à-vis the self, wherein the world is construed as collapsing into the self. Culminating in a naïve materialism, the first position is replaced by the second, a naïve idealism. In both instances, emptiness, the one of the self and the other of the world, challenges an harmonious relation between self and world, a relation which it was the original aim of both science and morality to affirm. Absolute trust, hence truth, threatens self-pulverization, the subjectivity of the self being consumed by objective relationships; absolute faith, hence goodness, threatens a vacuously expanded self confronting an insubstantial reality.

In my account, the good transcends the true while including it. Yet, in another sense, truth and goodness are mutually complementary. Indeed, the co-adaptation of the two constitutes a new dynamism, a further stage in the dialectical unfolding of freedom. Surely, the concrete universalization of freedom in a synthesis of truth and goodness is the culminating stage of thought. Progressively, the latter consummates itself by its progressive sympathetic identification with things, living creatures, persons. In attitudes of wonder, reverence, and the love of authentic kinship, the self empathically assimilates itself to these classes of objects which, reciprocally, reconstitute themselves in a fashion appropriate to their respective compositions.

An harmonious adjustment of self and world presupposes the

appropriate balance between goodness and truth. The former en-
closes the latter, which, however, presupposes it as immanent
ground; truth being enclosed, the terror of an infinitely empty
self and an infinitely empty world arises; conflict between the
two supervenes. Now, a new relationship, one of mutual co-
adaptation, emerges. In this phase, wherein self stands in relatedness to object, a dynamic relationship in which each is construed as itself dynamically constituted, one first glimpses one's
consummate freedom. For, where parity reigns between self and
other, no longer does one merely entrust oneself to the other—
self to object, affirming faith in its power to apprehend the latter;
object to self, affirming hope that the powers of the former will
conform to those of the latter. Now, self *and* other mold themselves in accordance with their respective powers. The artist
lovingly shapes his works and, in turn, is shaped by them; in
wonder he experiences this beauty. With reverence, the living
creature is lovingly beheld and acknowledged. In consummate
love of fellowship and kinship, persons experience the beauty
of their relationship with other persons. For, pre-eminently,
persons lovingly relate to one another—persons in relation, each
an authentic, self-determining agent. Things, living creatures,
persons: each compels relationships of varying modalities of
care. In each instance, the freedom of living relatedness unfolds
in new stages; at every point, the element of beauty resides within
an harmonious co-adaptation of self to object.

Unaware of numberless facets of the world even as it searches
to disclose those facets, the self dwells with itself unconsciously
as well as consciously.[11] By "world" I mean, broadly construed,
body in world. For no sharp distinction may be made between
bodily processes and world processes. Each is only a relatively
enduring configuration of actions within essentially the same
matrix. Moreover, associated with every body of sufficiently
complex organization is the self. Indeed, the self *is* that body
insofar as it is implicated in the world. It is the totality of feelings, perceivings, sensings, willings, desirings, believings. In a
word, it is the co-ordination of body's diverse intentions, its overall orientation toward the world; these intentions express modes
of discriminating the intertwinings of body processes with world
processes. Accordingly, in the exclusively material sense, body
is an abstraction; in the exclusively mental sense, self is an ab-

straction. Each prescinds from a more inclusive assemblage of
activities; each is hypostasized on the ground of those activities.
Hence, body is the locus of variegated activities which, *in their
subtler rhythms*, manifest themselves as self. The region mediat-
ing transition from the coarser to the more ethereal rhythms is,
in effect, the unconscious. Broadly expressed: body is the material locus of the self; correspondingly, the self is the mental locus
of the body. Insofar as bodily acts are intentional, and originate
within body in its narrower construal but point toward the world
in which body participates, one may therefore speak of the self.
For, in the last analysis, self expresses the animation of body;
it is at once the principle governing bodily organization and the
expression of that organization.

In consequence, neither body nor self may be conceived independently; sufficiently examined, each concept discloses itself
as entailing the other. Indeed, at bottom, body as a matrix of
intentional activities and self as the form of those activities are
one and the same. For form and matrix are indivisible. Self is
that unity in its reflexive aspect; body is that unity in its aspect
as the most intimate and proximate of reflection; world other
than body is that unity in its merely remote and less intimate
ingredients. In this sense, body and world form a continuum.
The relatively enduring crystallization of processes within this
continuum conventionally designated "my body" is but the locus
or seat of the self. However, insofar as body at its "periphery,"
so to speak, *is* the world—or, alternatively expressed, the world
exhibits singular nodes which are bodies—the self, equally, resides within the larger, more inclusive world. Indeed, the ultimate seat of every self is the *entire* world, with the qualification,
of course, that that world is apprehended (by the self) under the
perspective integrated by specific processes localized at critical
junctures within the world.

Accordingly, the idea of the self relating to itself as it relates
to objects in the modes of truth, goodness, and beauty (and love)
is equivalent to the idea that certain world regions are empowered to relate to themselves in their relationships to other world
regions. Briefly: the world exhibits privileged regions which
are reflexly endowed; by this character, the region is empowered
to activate certain latent contents. Indeed, every region is the
locus of conflict between forces resident within it which, in effect,

strive toward concealment of facets of that region and other forces within it which reflexively strive for disclosure. Yet, with Einstein, one may say: nature is subtle but not malicious.[12] Though elusive, nature is prone to re-present itself to itself. Thus doubling itself, it reflects into itself an Imago of itself. At bottom, this power of nature expresses its capacity for self-emendation, a tendency inhering within nature toward the efflorescence of its own hidden content.

Accordingly, when the self relates to its own relationship to the world, it is (in actuality) relating one region, its own region —the region it possesses as most intimately its own, or its body *qua* reflexive—to another region, the world *qua* non-reflexive. Truth and goodness express the form of this relationship. On the other hand, the more one manipulates the object toward which one orients oneself, the more one becomes aware that one is relating to that object as but the *manifestation* of its intrinsic powers. In beauty (and love), the self relates to its powers in their co-adaptability to the powers of what is other to it, as each set of powers potentiates the other into variegated expression. In this relationship, it becomes conscious of the interpenetration and mutual dependence of what it had initially conceived to be autonomous powers. In particular, as it passes from relating to mere inanimate powers to relating to the powers of living creatures, respecting the former and revering the latter, the self lays the groundwork whereby it may apprehend the intertwining of its own reflexivity with the reflexivity of the other. To be sure, this mode of relatedness culminates in the experience of one's own personhood as in profound relatedness to another person, as each indeed constitutive of the other. In this context, the phases of faith, hope, and love unfold anew.

Accordingly, the truth of the other is grasped as a representation of the interplay of the powers of both, a representation which is self-emending. For, in apprehending itself as the locus of powers, in part autonomous and in part woven of the other, the self becomes aware of confusions arising in its image of itself in relation to the other—confusions in which it imputes to itself powers properly belonging to the other, or conversely. At bottom, these distortions express nature's reluctance fully to reveal itself, its tendency, as it were, toward self-concealment. In effect, the self is un-conscious of the full truth regarding its own powers, or, for that matter, the powers of another person; and this un-consciousness develops in the course of the self-development of the self. To lay the groundwork for the self's articulation of those powers, evidently the collaboration of other persons is required. In the measure that such collaboration fails, the self distrusts the other, fearing an overpowering of him or by him. In effect, the self is not *heard* by the other, or, indeed, by its own self in its efforts to express itself adequately (i.e., as an adequate Imago of itself, a representation which is adequate to its intrinsic powers). In effect, the full truth of self or other is not experienced. Indeed, to experience that truth, one must have already been heard in one's effort to experience one's own truth, i.e., to frame an adequate representation to oneself of one's own powers.

Further, the goodness of the other is apprehended in the context of mutual deliberation regarding how *his* powers might more effectively be directed toward one's own gratification and, reciprocally—since, after all, this *is* a subphase of the phase of love—how one's own powers might analogously be directed toward gratification of his needs. Indeed, the giving of oneself up *in hope* to such deliberation guarantees that one selflessly affirm parity between the needs of the other and one's own needs. In this way, one endeavors so to relate one's own powers to the powers of the other that needs of either become ever-more-comprehensively satisfied. Since the relationship of love is already reciprocal, each person is active in this collaboration. Hence, perpetual adjudication, and the adjustment of the needs of each to each, typify this phase. As new needs arise, new deliberation supervenes. Together, the participants shape an ideal of peership in which this principle is affirmed: mutual loyalty will provide the conditions under which both parties may flourish with their fullest potentialities. Should this pact be violated, however, despair will reign; the essential goodness of the relationship will correspondingly diminish.

Finally, the framing of an adequate representation of the enmeshing of the strengths of persons is not the quintessential τέλος of the relationship of love. Nor is the using of each to the end that the other may be gratified, no matter how reciprocal this utilitarian purpose. Rather, the truthfulness and the goodness of love are but stages along the way toward the realization of beauty as pervading love. Only in this final subphase may both individuals dwell in vibrant peace. Only then may they experience that ecstasy of participation wherein, together, they orchestrate ever-new symbols of their union. In this context, neither self nor other can remove himself from their enraptured being-together. For each indelibly and unremittingly imprints the rhythms of his existence upon the other; each ornaments the themes of the lives of both with variations subtly and endlessly nuanced. For, in love, each person discloses his being, in its unity and in its entirety, by confronting two powers, his own and that of another; and he clarifies his being by joining himself to that other, by feeling the qualities of *his* existence in himself and of his own existence in the other. Through a relationship of mutual respect, tenderness, trust, understanding, hope, and loyalty, the power of each is enhanced. In every encounter, the self ceases to fragment experience, whether of himself or of the other. On the contrary, he enjoys its wholeness, its aliveness, and its unconditioned worth. In rhythmic alternation between inwardness and outwardness, a reverent bond to the other is established. One surrenders oneself to existence, to Rilke's "imperishable invisibility," [13] into which one has transfigured the visible and in which one always participates.

In the preceding pages, I have examined personal freedom in terms of a single idea: the correlation of the scriptural ideal with the classical ideal. Personal freedom, I have argued, consists essentially in the movement through stages specified by these ideals. Initially, the self possesses itself in relation to another in an attitude of faith. It aims so to apprehend the character of the other that it might root itself in a stable, lawful manifold. Thus freely giving itself up to truth, the self comes to own itself more securely. Yet, in the very act by which the self renounces all its desires save the need to attach itself to another in the latter's truthful character, the self becomes aware that the other is himself substantial and solid, a *durable* unfolding. Hence, it acquires a new attitude by which it complements its faith: namely, that of hope. For it may now hope that this substantial world is alterable in a way which would bring it into conformity with an ideal shaped from its own autonomous ruminatings. Accordingly, the self now possesses itself in an attitude of hope for the essential goodness of the other with respect to its own needs.

As soon as the self becomes aware of itself as a potential shaper of ideals and of the other as a manifold of lawful connections, it experiences *itself* as a manifold of lawful connections and the *other* as, in effect, the shaper (or, at least, the presenter) of ideals. In brief: it develops the power to apprehend both itself and the other as analogously constituted, hence capable of being brought into reciprocal dynamic relatedness. Thus, the self comes to possess itself in relation to another which (or who), immanently or explicitly, likewise comes to possess itself—each as reflexive activity, potential or actual. In consequence, self-possession in relation to another analogously conceived leads the self to an attitude of love. By this attitude, the beauty of an harmonious co-adaptation of powers, each to each, may be shaped.

Each symbolizing itself to the other, and the two in communion joining their symbolisms, these interwoven powers exhibit their own truth, goodness, and beauty. For, in the final analysis, personal freedom consists in the self giving itself to another self, and enjoying the mutuality of that giving: giving so that distrust, despair, and hate fall away; giving so that truth, goodness, and beauty be affirmed. For this to occur, ever-more-inclusive interpersonal relations must emerge, each grounded in the principles suggested by the correlations I have sketched, and ever-more-authentic communities must evolve: communities founded upon personal integrity, communities based on the idea of unity amid the diversity of its members, communities which embody in a collective lived experience the conditions whereby each member, unhampered, may search in the way I have proposed.

Granted: this way is arduous. Ultimately, it requires that one sacrifice one's narrower desires that one thereby unite oneself in the beauty of love to the eternal cosmic rhythms. Indeed, understood as God, the ground of these rhythms, construed as the divine witness to man's journey toward freedom, exhibits its own interwoven moments. In justice, God reveals His truth to man, that man has faith in His presence; in mercy, God reveals His goodness to man, that man have hope in His presence; in grace, God reveals His beauty to man, that man have love in His presence. Failure to undertake this adventure, in all its variegated aspects, jeopardizes faith, hope, and love. Should these ideals vanish, the quest for the true, the good, and the beautiful must be relinquished. The search for personal freedom must fail.

NOTES

1. For a psychological account of trust and hope in child development, see Erik Erikson, *Childhood and Society* (New York: Norton, 1950), chap. 7.

2. Leonard C. Feldstein, "The Human Body as Rhythm and Symbol: A Study in Practical Hermeneutics," *The Journal of Medicine and Philosophy*, 1, No. 2 (1976), 136–61.

3. Bendict de Spinoza, "On the Improvement of the Understanding," *Works of Spinoza*, trans. R. H. M. Elwes (New York: Dover, 1955), pp. 1–2.

4. Gabriel Marcel, *The Mystery of Being*, 2 vols. (Chicago: Gateway, 1951), Vol. II, chap. 10.

5. W. R. D. Fairbairn, *An Object Relations Theory of the Personality* (New York: Basic Books, 1954).

6. Alfred North Whitehead, *Process and Reality* (New York: Macmillan, 1929), chap. 2.

7. Ibid., p. 27.

8. Leonard C. Feldstein, "Toward a Concept of Integrity," *Annals of Psychotherapy*, Monograph Nos. 3 & 4, Vols. 1 & 2 (1961), 67–87.

9. For this etymologic discussion, see the relevant sources in Eric Partridge, *Origins* (London: Routledge and Kegan Paul, 1958) and *An Oxford Dictionary of English Etymology*, ed. C. Y. Onions (New York: Oxford, 1966).

10. See the fine discussion of the relationship between the true, the good, and the beautiful in Justus Buchler's theory of assertive, active, and exhibitive judgment in *Toward a General Theory of Human Judgment* (New York: Columbia University Press, 1951), chap. 2. See, too, the equally fine discussion of the relationship between self and world revealed in truth, goodness, and beauty by Albert Hofstadter, *Truth and Art* (New York: Columbia University Press, 1965), chaps. 5, 6, and 7.

11. See my discussions of body, mind, and unconscious in "Reflections on the Ontology of the Person," *International Philosophical Quarterly*, 9, No. 3 (September 1969), 313–41; and in "Bifurcated Psyche and Social Self: Implications of Freud's Theory of the Unconscious," *Person and Community*, ed. Robert J. Roth, s.j. (New York: Fordham University Press, 1975), pp. 43–62.

12. From a conversation of Einstein's, namely "Raffiniert ist der Herr Gott, aber boshaft ist er nicht." See *Albert Einstein: Philosopher–Scientist*, ed. Paul Arthur Schilpp, The Library of Living Philosophers 7 (Evanston, Ill.: The Library of Living Philosophers, Inc., 1949), p. 691.

13. See commentary on "The Angel" in Rainer Maria Rilke, *Duino Elegies* (New York: Norton, 1939), pp. 87–88.

5

Human Autonomy and Religious Affirmation in Hegel

QUENTIN LAUER, S.J.

FROM ONE POINT OF VIEW it could well seem that the religious philosophy of Hegel, whether in its abbreviated presentation in the *Phenomenology of Spirit* or in its more detailed articulation in the *Lectures on the Philosophy of Religion*, presents fewer difficulties for the informed reader than do other aspects of the "System." In it, to be sure, we do not find the convolutions which characterize the overall endeavor of the *Phenomenology*; nor are we confronted with the difficulty of keeping track of an extraordinarily intricate web of dynamic entailment, as we are in the *Science of Logic*. Even the *Aesthetics*, the *Philosophy of History*, the *History of Philosophy*, and the *Philosophy of Right* make more demands on the ingenuity—not to say the credulity —of the reader who would follow where Hegel's thought leads than does his religious philosophy.

From another point of view, however, that religious philosophy presents a seemingly insuperable difficulty, a paradox not readily resolved. How can Hegel present a religious philosophy at all? In the tradition, which began with Descartes, of progressively secularizing philosophical thought, no one is more insistent than Hegel on the autonomy of human reason, an autonomy which systematically denies that human reason is subject to any higher authority at all, not the authority of custom or tradition, certainly, not even the authority of the Church or the State. The very same Hegel, nevertheless, consistently refused to accept that the safeguarding of rational autonomy demanded progressive opposition to basic Christian faith, as did, for example, the triumphal rationalism of the Enlightenment. One could, of course, as Hegel did, repeatedly lecture on the philosophy of religion, without in any way compromising one's conviction that reason is completely autonomous. But could one's whole philosophy be as religious as Hegel's unquestionably is if one is convinced that there simply is no authority superior to reason?

The entire Hegelian endeavor is essentially religious in character. It is unified around one central theme, knowledge of the absolute, and the absolute, terminologically at least, is identified with God. More than that, the God with whom philosophy is occupied—or preoccupied—is identified with the God who is religion's concern. The pathway to knowledge of the absolute is described in the *Phenomenology*; the abstract framework in which the absolute which knowledge knows articulates itself is detailed in the *Logic*; the "empirical" verification of this articulation is put forth in the *History of Philosophy*, the *Aesthetics*, and the *Philosophy of Religion*; and the consequences of all this for the life of reason are enunciated in the *Philosophy of History* and the *Philosophy of Right*. Thus, the rational approach to the divine, which alone is "absolute," is for Hegel not a *part* of philosophy—not even its coping stone—it is the whole of philosophy, which seeks a comprehensive grasp of the whole of reality. Hegel is not saying, of course, that any philosopher, including himself, knows all reality; nor is he saying that any one philosophy, including his own, is adequate to the whole of reality. What Hegel *is* saying is that no knowledge of reality is truly knowledge unless what is known is situated in the framework of the totality, and that that framework is the system which philosophy has been developing into since its inception. What Hegel is also saying, however—along traditional theological lines—is that total knowledge makes sense only if its paradigm is God's absolute knowing, which is absolute precisely because its content is the absolute, i.e., God himself.

As Hegel sees it, then, philosophical thought requires religion if its content is to be adequately philosophical. The human experience which has God as its object is faith, and if thought is to be adequate to experience, its purview must include the faith experience; to ignore faith is to ignore its object and, thus, to condemn oneself to a truncated reflection on experience. Phi-

losophy will be indeed a *knowing* only if what it knows equals
what faith believes. It is for this reason that a reader who is
not familiar with the Christian religion—even with Christian
theology—will find it difficult if not impossible to fathom what
Hegel is saying.

None of this proves, of course, that Hegel was a Christian—
although he did throughout his life say that he was—but both
his language and his logic have their roots in the Christian religion, in Christian theology. What is more, Hegel's motivation
in insisting that both religion and philosophy are oriented to the
same absolute, such that his view of "scientific" philosophy could
be described as "faith seeking understanding," is not the desire
to rescue religion, to give it "rational" underpinnings. Rather,
it is his desire to rescue philosophy, which would be less than
universal science, would be severely limited in its range of inquiry, if the infinite object of religion were beyond its domain.
To put it rather simply: short of in some sense knowing all reality, philosophical knowing is not knowing in the full sense of the
term; and short of knowing God, philosophy does not know all
reality in any sense. Nor is this to say that, for Hegel, God must
be included in what is known if knowing is to be complete;
rather, he is saying that to know at all is to know God, that a
consciousness which is not a knowing of God is not knowledge,
and that to grow in knowledge is to grow in knowledge of God.
To put it another way: for Hegel it is inconceivable that philosophical knowing could be *having* bits and pieces of information, which may or may not be related to each other; there simply
are no unrelated bits of reality, and reality is truly known only
if it is known as totally interrelated. Paradigmatically, such a
knowing is divine, and its object too is divine. It is still true that
reason is autonomous, subject to no superior authority, for God
is Reason, Absolute Reason—or, to anticipate, "Absolute Spirit."

THE ROLE OF RELIGIOUS CONSCIOUSNESS

To show how all of this runs as a guiding thread throughout the
entire Hegelian endeavor would carry us too far afield. If, however, it can be shown that the dialectical movement of the *Phenomenology of Spirit* could never come to term if the march of
consciousness toward absolute knowing did not include the move-

ment of religious affirmation, we shall be able to see that religious affirmation—whatever that is to mean—cannot be absent from the systematic articulation of philosophical knowing. The *Phenomenology*, after all, is not simply a preliminary exercise which must be gone through before philosophizing can begin; its movement is the constant foundation of all that follows it.

If we are to understand the part which religion plays, according to Hegel's view, in the onward march of consciousness toward thoroughgoing knowledge, we must be aware that from beginning to end the *Phenomenology of Spirit* seeks to describe the progress of *human* spirit. At no point does the spirit whose development is being described become a disembodied consciousness, and it is precisely in the chapter on religious consciousness that this becomes abundantly clear; a disembodied consciousness simply could not be religious, only the human spirit can. What is more, religious consciousness is not presented as merely *one* of the stages in the spirit's advance, the penultimate one. Rather, the phenomenology of religious consciousness recapitulates the whole of the spirit's advance from minimal objective consciousness to self-conscious moral spirit before serving as a transition to the absolute knowing which is a thoroughgoing consciousness of self only because it is at the same time a consciousness of God. If human spirit is to know itself, it must know what it is to be spirit, and to know this is to know the paradigm of all spirit, God.

It is for this reason that the *Phenomenology*, which began as a "Science of the Experience of Consciousness," was forced along the route to recognize itself as a "Phenomenology of Spirit." At the very outset the consciousness which Hegel is examining begins to be aware that it does not belong to a mere realm of nature, where the mode of operation is that of causal efficacy. To be conscious is to act, not to be acted upon, and what this activity produces is precisely itself, consciousness. Explicit awareness may be slow in coming, but from the beginning it is inevitable that an activity which is not a being-acted-upon will recognize itself as spiritual activity. Even slower in coming is the spirit's awareness that it will not be adequate to itself as spirit until its activity is wholly spiritual, which is to say, in no way effected from outside itself. To call this a "consciousness of being all reality" is simply to say that to be conscious of any reality whatsoever is to be the autonomous center of the activity which is consciousness. Gradually this will also be to say that no reality is opaque to consciousness, provided that consciousness is not looked upon as the isolated consciousness of the single individual, and provided that "all reality" is not looked upon as the accumulation of bits and pieces of reality.

Here it is that the necessity of religious consciousness for the Hegelian phenomenological endeavor becomes clear. If the human spirit is completely autonomous in relation to its object, the spirit can, in that way at least, be said to be "absolute." That, however, is not enough for Hegel. Nor is it enough that "spirit" be concretely universalized by extension to *all* human consciousness, in time as well as space. To say that such a concretely universal spirit is "conscious of being all reality" is still to say that the "all" of which it is conscious is only formally, not concretely, universal. Thus, only if spirit's object is "absolute" is spirit itself absolute in the way in which Hegel intends. If the human spirit is essentially finite, as, I take it, Kant and Heidegger would have it, then its sphere of objectivity is also essentially finite. If, on the other hand, as Hegel would have it, the spirit's sphere of objectivity is infinite, then the spirit itself is essentially infinite. It is, then, essential to the integrity of human consciousness that it be religious, that it be consciousness of the absolute, the infinite, who is God. That, for Hegel, it is also essential to the integrity of human consciousness that the "of God" be taken as a subjective as well as an objective genitive, is a further point, which takes consciousness beyond the religious, as Hegel understands it; but to go beyond the religious is not, dialectically, to cease to be religious. As Hegel sees it, the autonomy of the human spirit demands that as self-conscious reason it must be both conscious of infinite reality and aware that this very consciousness is its own consciousness of itself. Only a reality which is spirit can be infinite; only a spirit which is infinite can be adequate to infinite reality; only if the human spirit is in some intelligible sense infinite can it be adequate to infinite reality.

Not even Kant and Heidegger, it would seem, would dispute the last statement. What both would dispute, however, is the one which precedes it. In Kant's view human reason in its speculative knowing—its knowing of what really is as opposed to what ideally ought to be—is limited to a finite field of objectivity.

Reason itself is essentially finite, since its function is merely regulative of what is presented in sense intuition and elaborated in the *a priori* categories of understanding. If there be an infinite, it is the object of faith alone, which is discontinuous with reason. Without going into the question of faith, Heidegger, for whom philosophy has nothing to say as to what is of faith, sees human consciousness as authentically human only when it is aware of its own essential finitude and of the finitude of the Being which is its "element." In opposition to Kant Hegel claims that the authentically human is characterized by thought and that, thus, a faith whose object would be beyond thought would not be authentically human. Against Heidegger he would argue that it is simply arbitrary to cling to a phenomenology of merely finite consciousness whose "element" is merely finite Being—and that it is a thoroughgoing phenomenology of human consciousness as spirit which demonstrates precisely this.

In saying this Hegel is not saying that the human spirit, either singly or collectively, is to be identified with God. What he is saying is that a consciousness of self which is not at the same time a consciousness of God is not in the full sense a consciousness of self, because it is not a consciousness of self as spirit in the full sense. Man is not God, but man's self-consciousness is man's God-consciousness. None of this, however, makes any sense if the God of whom man is conscious is some "Being" highest in the scale of being, a "supreme Being" or even an "absolute Being," who would be an object of human knowing only as an abstraction or a projection. Only a God who is "Spirit" is concrete, and for man to be conscious of himself as spirit is to be conscious of the concrete Spirit who is God, the knowledge of whom is a condition for any knowing's truly being knowing.

Against this background it is not difficult to see why, for Hegel, religious consciousness is an essential stage in the march toward adequate self-consciousness, which is identified with adequate knowing. Unless in the process of its development consciousness becomes religious, the self of which it is consciousness would be only partially a self, not all that the self as spirit is. It is the God who is present to consciousness in religion—however inadequate the form in which he is present—who reveals by his presence just what it is to be spirit, what it is to be activity without passivity, what it is to be truly autonomous. When Hegel says of this autonomous activity of the spirit that it is infinite he means what he says, but we should not be misled into thinking that he means it to be simply non-finite. The term is not negative in that sense at all. Rather, he is saying that the finite spirit is infinite, where "is" denotes neither identification nor attribution but "passing over to" or "becoming identical with," very much in the sense in which Aristotle says that in knowing the knower "becomes" the known. When finite spirit knows infinite Spirit— and only that is knowing in the full sense—it "becomes" the Spirit it knows.

HEGEL'S GOD

When all of this has been said, of course, it could still be argued —as Kojève, Kaufmann, and Findlay do argue—that the "absolute Spirit" of which Hegel speaks need not be God, that it need only be the concretely universalized human spirit, something like the Feuerbachian projection of the perfectly human. If, in fact, all we had to go on were the *Phenomenology of Spirit*, it might be difficult to prove this argument wrong. It is, nevertheless, equally difficult to see how a non-divine absolute would make sense, even if we were to confine ourselves to the *Phenomenology*. Nor is it easy to maintain that Hegel is simply speaking of a concretely universalized human spirit, which neither Feuerbach nor Marx claimed he was doing; they said, rather, that that is all he could legitimately do, and that thus he was wrong in what he did do. If, further, we look at the whole of Hegel's philosophy, such an interpretation seems completely incompatible with his emphasis on the so-called "ontological argument," of which the *Science of Logic* is a prolonged elaboration, and which occupies a central position in the *Lectures on the Philosophy of Religion*, the *Lectures on the Proofs for the Existence of God*, and in the Introduction to the *Lectures on the History of Philosophy*.

In any event, whether or not for Hegel religious consciousness bespeaks a consciousness of God, it clearly bespeaks an object which transcends mere finite human spirit. It is clear, too, that in Hegel's view only a "divine" spirit is concretely universal and that only for such a consciousness is there no conflict between the world of reality (objectivity) and the world of spirit (subjectivity), precisely because they are one and the same world. We might say, either a consciousness of divine Spirit or no adequate comprehension of reality. One may opt for the second member of the disjunction, but it is difficult to see how one would be following Hegel in doing so. It is true, of course, that spirit needs the mediation of a world of reality in order to know itself as spirit—hence the "System"—but the world of reality will make spirit known to itself only if the world itself is a revelation of Spirit. The human spirit can see itself as the autonomous source of the world (all reality) it knows only if it *re-creates* a world which the divine Spirit *creates*.

Up to this point, it might well seem, religious thinkers could find Hegel's exposition congenial to their own thinking. In fact, however, many religious thinkers, with Kierkegaard in the lead, have been quick to point out that Hegel goes too far. It is all very well, they say, to contend that a consciousness which does not ultimately have God as its object is a truncated consciousness and that it is religious consciousness which expressly makes God the ultimate content of consciousness. Still, the argument continues, to go further with Hegel and to insist that even religious consciousness is not adequate to its object, that to believe in God and to worship him is not enough, since he also must be *known* by autonomous, self-conscious reason, is to downgrade religion and to rationalize God. The reaction is understandable but perhaps not justifiable. First of all, Hegel is speaking of the *phenomenon* of religious consciousness, i.e., in any of the forms in which it has yet manifested itself. In all of these, Hegel finds, although the God who is the object of religion is the Absolute, ultimately—in Christian religion—Absolute Spirit, still the form under which he is present to religious consciousness is the form of "representation," which *stands for* God but is not the very *presence* of God in thought. God, then, can be present in thought only if thought itself is absolute, if it is "absolute knowing," which would seem to be saying that religion is swallowed up in what Hegel considers to be philosophical thought. This, however, would be true only if faith ceased to be faith once it had achieved a rational grasp of its own content; and it might furthermore well be true that rational thought could not have God as its content, the way it does throughout Hegel's *Logic*, if it did not constantly have faith as its underpinning. If this be the case, then philosophical knowing neither swallows up nor cancels out religious consciousness; it simply transforms religion into an explicit consciousness of its own implications. In any event what Hegel has to say about developing religious consciousness and of its necessity in the story of developing spirit will make a great deal of sense against the backdrop of the present interpretation.

From another point of view it might be argued, with Feuerbach, that the ultimate logic of Hegel's position demands a humanizing of the divine, reducing God to the only kind of object he can be if he is to be the object of human thought. But, again, it could be argued with equal, if not greater, cogency that Hegel's position involves a divinizing of the human in that it insists that a human consciousness of self which falls short of being a consciousness of God is not consciousness of the integral self. Not until we have gone through the history of religious consciousness as Hegel presents it, with its culmination in "absolute knowing," will it be possible to choose between the alternative interpretations.

THE PROGRESS OF RELIGIOUS CONSCIOUSNESS

In an effort to follow Hegel, then, as he engages in a phenomenology of religious consciousness, we can say in a general sort of way that a religious human consciousness consists in an awareness of a divine being (whatever "divine" will ultimately mean) which transcends both man and man's world and is, thus, "absolute." Initially this awareness is minimal, no more than a sort of intuitive affirmation of a vague being, out there, which is dependent on nothing and on which all depends, an all-pervasive presence—"the Absolute." Now, just as the whole *Phenomenology* consists in a progressive and tortuous concretization in thought of an originally indeterminate minimal consciousness, and just as the *Logic* presents the progressive thinking determination of an originally purely abstract being, so the phenomenology of religious consciousness consists in a progressive elaboration of the implications contained in the initial awareness of "the Absolute."

The process, as Hegel describes it, might aptly be designated an *ascensio mentis ad Deum*, wherein the ascent of individual man recapitulates the slow ascent of social man through history.

Roughly the process is divided into three stages: religion of nature, religion of art, and religion of revelation.

(*a*) Religion of Nature: Nature, which stands over against man and embodies a force which is sometimes benign sometimes hostile, reveals to man a more than nature itself. This it does with a minimum of intervention on the part of the human spirit, with a minimum of thought. The God (or gods) of this stage is simply a felt need if man is to cope with nature, an absolute to be invoked or placated. We can call it the Absolute as "force."

(*b*) Religion of Art: The activity of human spirit takes over as man transcends nature by consciously—and self-consciously—producing works of art which reveal at once a more than themselves and a more in man's consciousness of the Absolute. In the work of art there is a divine presence, but it is put there by man. The God of this stage can be called the Absolute as "beauty."

(*c*) Religion of Revelation: Man has gradually become aware that his God is Spirit, one who previously spoke to man through nature, then through the products of man's own creative activity, and now speaks to man in a language which the mind of man can grasp. At this stage the divine Spirit is truly present to man. Spirit speaks to spirit, and not through sensible or imaginary embodiments. The Absolute here is recognized as Spirit—who "speaks."

Even in this last stage, however, the divine Spirit is present to man only in the "word" which Spirit speaks. The word, it is true, is the most spiritual of all instruments, but it is still only an instrument. Only when the divine Word "becomes flesh" is the divine Spirit truly present among men; and only when the "Word become flesh" dies can the divine Spirit be present in the spirit of man. It is thus that Hegel interprets those words of the Fourth Gospel "The Spirit shall teach you all truth"; the Spirit will not merely speak *to* man, he will speak *in* man. Thus the "absolute knowing" in which Hegel's *Phenomenology* culminates (to be explicated in the subsequent "System") is the actual presence of the divine Spirit in man which follows upon the death of the *individual* God-man.

To expand these broad outlines to include the details of the process as Hegel presents it would be to rewrite the *Lectures on the Philosophy of Religion* or, at the very least, the long seventh chapter of the *Phenomenology*. Suffice it to say that Hegel does touch all the bases in going from the vague image of "Light" which characterizes Zoroastrianism to the purified "religion of the spirit" which he considers German Lutheranism to be. What is important to note is that Hegel sees the process of developing religious consciousness (both individual and historical) as an organic continuum with its own logic, parallel to the overall continuous process of consciousness journeying by its own efforts from minimal sensation to "absolute knowing." It is important, too, to note that for Hegel consciousness will never reach the goal of the overall journey if it does not make the religious journey. Only if the God of whom man is conscious is progressively spiritualized will man progressively recognize the true spirituality of his own consciousness. The human consciousness which is conscious of itself as thoroughly spiritual in its activity is by the same token conscious of its own autonomy, since to be spiritual is to be not acted upon. In relation to the world of objectivity over against man, this means that he actively makes it his own—"appropriates" it—re-creates it.

HIGHLIGHTS OF THE MOVEMENT

To appreciate the role which Hegel assigns to religious consciousness in this process of spiritualization we can, without reproducing all the details, consider the highlights of man's progressive awareness of the divine. It should be noted at the outset, however, that Hegel does not see the movement as one from individual to corporate consciousness; it is integral to religious consciousness that it be from the beginning corporate. It should be noted, too, that its forward movement is constituted by an "appropriation" at each successive level of what is "represented" at the immediately preceding level. This "appropriation" is the active "doing" of self-consciousness in its progressive awareness of selfness. Primitive man represents to himself a divine power "out there," a divinity which, the more primitive the representation, the more its "attributes" are what they are because they are "attributed" to it by man. Thus, the god who is made known to man in the works of nature is, so to speak, a "natural" being, a "first cause," a "force," a "supreme being," the source of nature's workings. When man's spirit begins to intervene in the process by creating the work of art which embodies man's god, then the god himself begins to be revealed as spirit. The revelation of the god as spirit and the revelation of man's own spirituality run a parallel course, both moving from vagueness to concreteness. As the art work becomes less and less a material thing "out there" and becomes more and more the "acting out" of religious mystery, the human performer becomes more and more aware of his own importance as the "god-bearer" and, thus, of the presence of divinity in human artistic activity, which is at the same time religious activity.

Up to this point, Hegel contends, it is inevitable that man should represent divinity to himself as a plurality of individual gods, a plurality which, again, is progressively united in the vague community of divine being through the medium of self-conscious poetic expression—an artistic activity suffused with spirit. The poetic expression of divinity-consciousness reaches its high point in Greek tragedy. There can be no doubt that Hegel sees the progress of art from the primitive to the sophisticated as a developing spiritualization of artistic activity. There can be little doubt, although he does not say so expressly, that he sees all poetry (perhaps all art) as in its original development essentially religious, i.e., as the progressively more self-conscious expression of a *people's* religious awareness.

However high Hegel's esteem of Greek tragedy as an art form, he does recognize it as a point of no return in religious consciousness. Like Plato he sees the legendary gods of tragedy (inherited from Greek mythology) as essentially non-gods with their all-too-human foibles. It was necessary, then, that these gods be cut down to size in comedy, revealed as what they were, substitutes for the unified divinity of the Absolute who is Spirit. It is the very irreverence of comedy, then, which ushers in the sublime ideals of "the beautiful," "the true," "the good" celebrated by Socrates and Plato, given an identifiable divine form in the "thought thinking thought" of Aristotle's *Metaphysics*, his "divine science." With this, the way to religious–philosophical monotheism is opened. Once more the paths of a God becoming spiritualized and of man becoming conscious of his own spirit run parallel. Ultimately, only a God who is himself totally spirit could satisfy the demands of a human consciousness gradually becoming more fully aware of its own spirituality. To such a God the Greek spirit could not attain. As Hegel sees it, only a God who actively, self-consciously reveals himself to man as

Spirit can satisfy man's spirit. For such a God the Greek spirit, with an infusion of Judaic revelation, was ready; Christian history could begin; God could reveal himself to man and thus reveal to man what man himself is. Even God, however, could not do this merely through the instrumentality of human words; only through a revelation which is incarnation could God do it. Thus, for Hegel, it is necessary that there be the leap to Christian religion, to Christian revelation, a revelation of what it is for God to be man and, therefore, of what it is for the human to become divine, of what it is for man to be truly man, the "god-bearer," truly spirit.

HEGEL'S "THEOLOGY"

When Hegel reaches the Christian religion, which he considers to be the culmination of the progressive development of religious consciousness, affording the highest degree of self-consciousness which religion as such can, he is impelled to interpret it in such a way that it elucidates all that any religion can regarding the reality of human consciousness as "spirit." For Hegel Christian religion is "absolute religion," in the sense that religious consciousness simply cannot go beyond it: there is no religious "beyond." If there is a consciousness of the absolute beyond Christian religious consciousness, it must be, so to speak, a suprareligious consciousness. Before going into the question of such a suprareligious consciousness, however, Hegel seeks to interpret "spiritually" five major themes of Christian revelation, with a view to showing that the "mysteries" in question when properly—"spiritually"—understood constitute a revelation of consciousness as spirit and of self-consciousness as a consciousness of being spirit (of what it is to be spirit). In the context of Hegel's elaboration it would seem that "spiritual interpretation" is roughly equivalent to "demythologization," in which the language of the revelation is stripped of its inevitable metaphorical character in order to uncover its true meaning. The five mysteries which Hegel has chosen to interpret thus are Incarnation, Trinity, Creation, the Fall, and Redemption.

Hegel has quite obviously chosen well. It might, of course, be argued that the themes of Creation and Fall—even of some sort of Redemption—are not uniquely Christian. If, however, the mysteries as interpreted are meaningful only in an incarnational context, as Hegel claims they are, then all five themes are uniquely Christian. The Incarnation is, clearly, the central mystery of Christianity, not only in the sense that from it Christianity derives both its name and its character, but also in the sense that the other four are intelligible from a Christian point of view only as making possible an explication of Incarnation. The trinity of "Persons" in God is necessary if God's entry into human history is to be possible at all. Creation is necessary if there is to be a human history into which God can enter. The movement away from God in the Fall is necessary if there is to be a reason for Incarnation. Redemption is necessary if Incarnation is to be an effective presence of God in human history.

1) *Incarnation*. In Christian religious consciousness the Incarnation is a uniquely concrete union of the divine and the human in the individual God-man, whom history calls Jesus and whom Christians call the Christ. According to Hegel Jesus Christ is the most totally human of all humans precisely because he is divine, the model of the integrally human, because only the man who is more than merely natural man is integrally human, spiritual. Gone, says Hegel, is the fragmented divinity of the Greek pantheon whose only unified intelligibility is the abstract unity of divine "substance," a sort of "class" to which all the "gods" belong—or from which, perhaps, all are derived. This sort of substantial unity bespeaks no unity of self-consciousness either on the side of divinity or on the side of a humanity related to the divine. The incarnation of the God-man Jesus Christ reconciles divine substance and human self-consciousness. In Jesus the divine substance "empties" itself (the Pauline κένωσις) becoming a concrete human self and thus revealing a concrete selfhood in God. It is thus that Jesus reveals *that* God is Spirit—not merely substance or "supreme being"—and reveals too *what* it is for man to be essentially spirit. As Hegel sees it, however, precisely because in Jesus Christ God is sensibly present in bodily form, Jesus is not yet fully *who* he is; his body must die that his Spirit may live in the Christian community.

2) *Trinity*. The God of the philosophers, whether of Plato, Aristotle, or Plotinus, whether the deistic God of the Enlightenment—or even the God of Kant, Jacobi, and Fichte, to whom philosophical thought cannot attain—is no more than an ab-

stract "supreme being." The concrete God of Christianity is a trinity of "Persons," revealed, not in the Incarnation alone, but in the Incarnation and the descent of the Spirit consequent on the death of the God-man. Because the Spirit is present in and to the human spirit—in the community—the en-spirited community can see the man Jesus as the human revelation of the divine. The divinity revealed in and through Jesus is triune: the divinity *in itself*, the Father; the divinity in the individual Jesus, the Son; the divinity in the believing *community*, the Spirit. Herein there is a reconciliation of transcendence and immanence only because the transcendent Father is immanent in the Son, whose Spirit is immanent in the community, extended in both space and time. To grasp conceptually (*begreifen*) the divine reality, human consciousness finds that its awareness of God is of a God articulated into a related triplicity (Trinity). To articulate this triplicity in language, the Christian community employs names to designate the members of this triplicity. Thus, the names—Father, Son, Spirit—are metaphors based on human relationships. The distinctions of persons are meaningful only if they are at the same time grasped as non-distinctions in a reality of dynamic movement, self-movement, with which only "speculative thought" can ultimately come to grips. When religion, even "absolute" religion, gives names to the "persons" of this trinity, it is articulating this self-movement, which is Spirit—God as Spirit. The "moments" of this spiritual movement, says Hegel in an effort to transcend the metaphors of "names," are "being," "knowledge," and "love," united in the dynamic unity of self-comprehension which he calls "concept," thus foreshadowing the dynamic unity of totally interrelated reality and totally interrelated conceptual thought.

Having given his "spiritual" interpretation of the Incarnation as the movement of God's supreme self-revelation, a movement which extends through the whole earthly life of the God-man culminating in his physical death and resurrection whereby the Spirit comes to dwell in and animate the community, Hegel has been able to interpret the Trinity as self-movement in the interior life of God. This, then, enables him further to interpret a series of figurative terms which occur in Christian theological speculation in the language of the "concept" understood as a movement of "concrescence." "Creation," "Fall," and "Redemption" are themselves figurative terms, and in their explication theology employs other figurative terms which demand interpretation.

3) *Creation.* If the term "create" is taken to mean "make out of nothing," a making which is, as ordinarily understood, in the mode of causal efficacy, Hegel contends, then it is a "representational" (metaphorical) term designating God's spiritual activity in relation to the world's coming-to-be. This divine activity Hegel sees as a "knowing"—with its distinctively Hegelian overtones of "conceiving," which is comprehending by concretely putting together. The *Phenomenology* has sought to establish that all knowing is a knowing of self. Thus even God's knowing is a knowing of himself, and his knowing of the world is the explicitation of that self-knowledge in conceiving and thus bringing into being a world as the outward expression of God's own being. If human knowing is to be truly a knowing, then, it must be analogous to divine knowing, such that man in knowing his world knows himself and in knowing himself knows his world in a manner parallel to God's "creating." Creation, then, is the work of reason knowing, bringing into being and putting together what it knows. The world is the creation of divine Reason and is, thus, rational, revealing both in its spatial dimensions (nature) and in its temporal dimensions (history) reason as its source. By the same token the world grasped in human knowing is the re-creation of the world in human reason; the primordial unity of divine creation having been fragmented by the abstractive activity of scientific understanding is put together again by the creative (re-creative) activity of reason. Thus, human re-creative reason whereby the human reason knows itself is a sharing in the divine Reason whereby God knows himself.

4) *The Fall.* If it is true to say that the phenomenon of the human is a sharing in the divine, then it would seem reasonable to say also that human failure to express the divine is a falling away from that which makes the human to be integrally human. This, however, is not the way Hegel interprets the biblical account of the Fall. Rather, he sees the creation of man as initially man's mere being in the world and man's "innocence" as no more than his lack of responsibility for that world. Becoming responsible, then, is the movement which explicates creation; negatively expressed: it is the loss of "innocence." It is worth

noting that the German term for "in-nocence" (*Schuldlosigkeit*) is literally translated "faultlessness," a state which is proper to *nature*, not to *spirit*. Thus, if man is to pass from nature to spirit, nature must, so to speak, be "faulted"; fault becomes a condition for the movement from being *innocent* to being *good*. In this context the "tree of knowledge of good and evil" becomes the symbol of that knowledge which puts an end to innocence; the "fruit" which the first couple, as comprising all humanity, pluck and eat is the symbol of that self-knowledge which is the beginning of responsibility for a world of reality as known; and the "Angel of Light" (Lucifer) who opens the eyes of humanity's first couple symbolizes the awakening of consciousness which will ultimately culminate in the authentic life of spirit. It is all one movement, but at the same time it is but the first faltering steps of a larger overall movement. Thus, the Fall itself is the first step toward reconciliation; to know good as good and evil as evil is to be on the road to reconciliation, and the *felix culpa* is truly "happy" because it sets the scene for "redemption."

5) *Redemption.* Looked at from the side of God, "creation" is not an instantaneous act but a movement wherein man, who has come into being in a world of reality which is over against him and unknown by him, makes that world of reality his own by progressively sharing in the divine creative activity. Looked at from the side of man, that same process can be looked at as the one overall movement of "redemption." Here, once more, "incarnation" becomes central; incarnation *is* redemption. The abstract being of a God who is seen only as "Creator" is in time expressed in the concreteness of a human self-consciousness. Creation, then, is the beginning of externalization of an otherwise abstract God, and incarnation is the further concretization of a God who takes upon himself human self-consciousness in order that man may take to himself concrete God-consciousness and thus be redeemed. Incarnation, however—and thus creation, too—is not complete until the individual God-man dies physically in order to rise spiritually in the community which is to live his life.

Whether or not this Hegelian systematization of salvation history, in which all events are "moments" of one connected movement, can prove fruitful in coming to terms with religious mystery we can leave to the theologians—or historians of theology. That, despite its sometimes quite obviously fanciful exegesis, it tells us a great deal about Hegel's conception of the progressive "spiritualization" of human reality is unmistakable. It is also clear that Hegel means to be taken seriously when he articulates the moments of this process "religiously." How religious all this really is is disputed by many—on both sides of the religious divide. Secularists like Marx and Feuerbach see the whole thing as illegitimate precisely because Hegel takes God and the divinization of man seriously. Secularists like Kojève, Kaufmann, and Findlay legitimize Hegel's account by seeing in it the complete secularization of what is only metaphorically called "religious consciousness." Religionists—and their name is legion —tend to condemn Hegel because he has destroyed religion altogether. No one, however, denies that Hegel has provided us with a fascinating, grandiose, and in some ways compelling panoramic vision of human development.

Without denying a certain cogency to the "secularist" interpretation of Hegel's account—at least of the one contained in the *Phenomenology*—we can turn now to the two principal objections raised by religionists. The first, which was raised by Kierkegaard, is quite simply that the account is too systematically coherent. By it Hegel has so rationalized religion—and Christianity in particular—that it has ceased to be religion at all; a faith which has been transformed into rational knowledge is no longer faith. A first answer to this objection might be to give the account all over again. It is scarcely "rational" in the narrow sense implied by Kierkegaard—Hegel is not a "rationalist" in that sense at all. Mysteries do not cease to be mysteries, nor does faith cease to be faith, in a systematic framework of interconnection wherein both belief and what is believed have significance only in relation to the ongoing development of the human spirit.

A somewhat more sophisticated answer to the same objection might be to point out that Hegel was neither the first nor the last to avow that *fides* must seek *intellectum* if it is to be adequate as *fides*. It is also true, of course, that Kierkegaard was neither the first nor the last to insist that faith must avoid doing precisely that. The point is that Hegel has quite firmly inserted his philosophical enterprise into the tradition of Augustine, Anselm, Bonaventure, and Thomas Aquinas, for none of whom was it a degradation of faith to seek at least a limited understanding. It might be argued that Hegel's fault lay in seeking an *unlimited* understanding, a totally *rational* account, but this too hangs on the meaning of "rational." What Hegel has done is not so much to rationalize faith as to broaden the concept of reason so as to embrace faith. His attempt, then, to articulate faith in rational terms is an attempt to show it as a continuous dynamic movement with its own inner logic, a logic which is not different from that of man's spiritual development, his growth toward rational autonomy. It is true that in so doing Hegel has given to what are termed the "mysteries" of faith the inevitability of rational process, but he does not fail to explain what this means. He first distinguishes between "mystery" (*mysterion*) and "secret" (*Geheimnis*). Mystery, then, is a profound truth in which is revealed to man what his relationship to the divine truly is. Secret, on the other hand, is what is hidden from man, preventing him from knowing either himself or God. In this context it is the function of reason to embrace mystery—the mystery of man in God and God in man. "Rational process," too, is not the process of formal logical-entailment; rather, it is the process of organic growth, continuity of movement. The content of religion given in faith grows to maturity; faith itself grows to maturity; and so do the "faithful."

The second objection is not completely different from the first, even though, perhaps, it is more widespread. It is specifically directed against the place accorded to religion in the *Phenomenology of Spirit*, but it involves the complaint that the Hegelian "System" has become a substitute for genuine religion. If, it is claimed, religion is the penultimate step in the march of human spirit to the complete possession of itself in "absolute knowing," then religious consciousness is "superseded by," "swallowed up in," absolute knowing. The objection is serious and has its plausibility. It is true, of course, that Hegel does speak of religion as being *aufgehoben* in absolute knowing. It is true, too, that *aufheben* is usually translated by "supersede" (or, sometimes, "transcend"), but Hegel is hardly to be condemned on the basis of an inadequate translation of this key term in the language of dialectic. He himself takes pains to point out that the term *aufheben*, even in ordinary German usage, has three meanings: "cancel," "retain," and "raise up." As a *dialectical* term, he then tells us, it has all three meanings at once, each inextricably bound up with the others. Thus, to say that religion is *aufgehoben* in absolute knowing is to say that the latter "cancels" (or "eliminates"), not religion, but the inadequacy of the "form of representation." At the same time absolute knowing "retains" the same absolute content of religion, such that without the retention of religious consciousness knowing would have no absolute content; nor would it know what it is to be "absolute." Furthermore, absolute knowing "raises" religion to a level of realization of all that religion implies. Because, as Hegel sees it, "thinking" characterizes human spirit at the highest pitch of intensity, then man's relationship to the highest, to God, must be a thinking-relationship. Religion, we might say, is most truly religion when it is thought. It should be pointed out, however, that the "thinking" in question is not merely theoretical. Because, he says, religious consciousness "thinks" God under the guise of "figurative representation" (religious metaphor), it can "unite" itself to God only in a subsequent activity, that of "cult." Absolute knowing, then, by canceling the form of representation can combine the two steps into one; it is at once a "knowing of" and a "dynamic unification with" God. Absolute knowing does not "swallow up" religion; it "completes" religion, makes it to be what religion truly is. If all consciousness is ultimately self-consciousness, then the God-consciousness of religion is ultimately self-consciousness. This is the Hegelian version of Spinoza's *amor intellectualis Dei*, where the "of God" is to be taken as both an objective and a subjective genitive— man knows God, and thus God is the *object* of his knowing; man knows God, and thus the human *subject* is divinized in the knowing.

It might still be objected, of course, that to designate the profoundest relationship of the human spirit to the divine Spirit as "knowing" is a deceptive use of terms. Perhaps it is. Perhaps there is a better term to designate that spiritual activity of man's which is at once most autonomous and most characteristically divine in man. If there be such, I am sure Hegel would raise no objection. Philosophy is not a matter of words—nor is religion.

6

Human Autonomy
and Political Authority

VINCENT M. COOKE, S.J.

IN HIS BOOK *In Defense of Anarchism*, Robert Paul Wolff has written one of the most thought-provoking essays in contemporary radical political philosophy.[1] I believe that Wolff's arguments are wrong and that anarchism is indefensible. But an accomplished philosopher and distinguished Kantian scholar such as Wolff does not make mistakes without at the same time saying a great deal which is true and challenging others to clarify and defend their own points of view.

Wolff writes about the concepts of authority, autonomy, reason, obedience, legitimacy, power, and the state. He concludes that the notion of a just state is a contradiction in terms and that the only morally justifiable political position is philosophical anarchism. I shall try to show that Wolff has misconceived the cluster of political concepts which he investigates. A proper understanding not only will show that Wolff's argument for anarchism fails, but also will provide a basis for a rational justification of political authority, i.e., a solution to the problem which Wolff has called the fundamental problem of political philosophy.

I

Wolff's position can easily be summarized. He begins with an analysis of the concept of authority. Authority, he says, is "the right to command, and, correlatively, the right to be obeyed."[2] Wolff distinguishes it from power, which is the ability to compel compliance, through either the use or the threat of force. The state is defined as the group of persons who have the right to exercise supreme authority within a territory.[3] The obedience which authority has a right to claim is a compliance simply because the authority commands. If I do what an authority commands because I am convinced by arguments or otherwise that what is commanded is the right thing to do, this is not obedience, according to Wolff. "Obedience is not a matter of doing what someone tells you to do. It is a matter of doing what he tells you to do *because he tells you to do it*."[4]

The analysis of the concept of authority is followed by a corresponding analysis of the concept of autonomy. Autonomy, according to Wolff, is man's basic moral obligation. It consists in taking responsibility for his actions and determining for himself what he ought to do. Taking responsibility, Wolff observes, "lays upon one the additional burdens of gaining knowledge, reflecting on motives, predicting outcomes, criticizing principles, and so forth."[5] The main point is that the autonomous man is not subject to the will of another. "He may do what another tells him, but not because he has been told to do it."[6] "Taking responsibility for one's actions means making the final decisions about what one should do."[7]

Given the above conceptual analysis, Wolff simply concludes that there is no way in which authority can be reconciled with autonomy, and that, therefore, the concept of a just state "must be consigned the category of the round square, the married bachelor, and the unsensed sense-datum."[8] The only reasonable political belief is philosophical anarchism.

> The defining mark of the state is authority, the right to rule. The primary obligation of man is autonomy, the refusal to be ruled. It would seem, then, that there can be no resolution of the conflict between the autonomy of the individual and the putative authority of the state. Insofar as a man fulfills his obligation to make himself the author of his decisions, he will resist the state's claim to have authority over him. That is to say, he will deny that he has a duty to obey the laws of the state *simply because they are laws*. In that sense, it would seem that anarchism is the only political doctrine consistent with the virtue of autonomy.[9]

Wolff buttresses his case with a lengthy discussion of the ways in which various kinds of democracy have attempted to reconcile authority and autonomy, and, in Wolff's view, have failed.[10] For our purposes, however, there is no need to rehearse Wolff's arguments against democracy since what he says is in effect simply a corollary of the positive argument elaborated above.

II

There is much in Wolff's position which seems to be right. Man's fundamental obligation is, indeed, to assume responsibility for his actions, and this means governing and shaping his own life in terms of reasons which he himself recognizes and accepts as morally cogent. At least this much seems to have been proven by Kant when he isolated the categorical imperative as the formal element in all moral action. In this respect Kant made a major advance over the received tradition of moral philosophy.

Before Kant, insofar as philosophers discerned a formal element in morality at all, they did so in terms of the most general maxims such as "Do good and avoid evil" or "Follow the dictates of right reason." But such maxims are only ambiguously described as formal elements of morality. They usually presuppose what I shall call a spectator account of morality.[11] Morality is looked upon as a set of true practical judgments, which are indeed to be appropriated by a subject, but which otherwise stand over against the subject. The formal element of such a set of judgments is simply the most general principle which can be seen to be instantiated in each of the more specific judgments which make up the content of the moral system.

But Kant is giving, not a spectator, but a performative, account of morality. Being moral is something which human beings *do* or fail to *do*. The formal element, with which Kant was concerned, is the formal element of the activity of being a moral agent. Thus, Kant's insight, capsulated in the categorical imperative, is that the indispensable element in moral activity is governing one's actions by reasons which (and this is analytically true of what counts as a reason) can be explicated in terms of principles which will apply to all relevantly similar agents in relevantly similar circumstances. To be a moral agent is to be autonomous in precisely this sense. I assume responsibility for my actions by basing them on reasons which I judge to be acceptable. Activity in accord with the categorical imperative is thus a necessary, even if not sufficient, condition of moral activity.[12]

Kant has made clear that being moral is a matter of activity and not merely of behavior. Behavior is something which happens, which is caused and can be manipulated. Activity is the product of rational deliberation and choice. It was this difference which the spectator accounts of morality tended to obscure. Heteronomy is the refusal to accept responsibility for one's actions by evaluating the reasons and alternative courses of action available to the agent. It, of course, admits of degrees. Most men, at some time, refuse responsibility in some areas of their lives, and the completely heteronomous individual is unlikely to be encountered outside of a mental hospital. To employ Kant's colorful rhetoric: it is rare indeed that humanity is completely lost. The main point, however, is that it is only insofar as one is autonomous that the possibility of moral action exists, precisely because autonomy is the condition of the possibility of rational activity at all.

Thus, the first condition of morality is that a man assume responsibility to deliberate about the reasons which will guide his actions. However, he does not deliberate about reasons in an historical, cultural, or metaphysical vacuum. There was a tendency in Kant sometimes to do this, and it led to the comment that to attempt to get substantive morality out of the categorical imperative is like trying to get milk out of a he-goat.[13] When I act for a reason, I set a goal or purpose for my activity. It is unintelligible to speak of an activity without an end. The purpose will be achieved either in the activity itself or in something to which the activity leads. My activity is rational insofar as it achieves my purposes; it is irrational insofar as it defeats my own ends. A major part of our moral deliberation consists in efforts to discern precisely where our true interest lies. Morality is thus ultimately grounded on anthropology, on our constant and never completely successful efforts to clarify and articulate man's interests and needs.

From this point of view, Wolff's position, briefly sketched but not argued for in his latest book, *The Autonomy of Reason*, could be restructured as suggesting that man's ultimate interest is in a rational community in which the participants deliberate about whatever more substantive principles they may wish to agree upon.[14] Wolff, to be sure, does not appeal to man's interests, and would object to my appeal to anthropology as an illicit deduction of normative principles by *a posteriori* means. Still, Wolff admits that he has so far been unsuccessful in trying to construct his needed transcendental deduction of the principle of rational community. One reason for this failure may be that such a deduction is impossible. All I can say here is that it seems to me the essence of rationality that all substantive morality be ultimately grounded in man's interests and needs, though I acknowledge that an elaborate defense of this position remains as a future task.

Robert Johann has argued that man's overriding and transcendent interest is an interest in community.[15] In this respect, by a very different route, he arrives at a conclusion very similar to Wolff's. I believe that Johann has proved that man has an interest in community. I am less certain, for reasons which would only distract us here, that his argument proves that community is man's overriding and transcendent interest. It seems to me that man has many interests and needs, and that one of the very important ones is community.

My argument thus far leads to the conclusion that Wolff is right in his stress on the importance of autonomy. A man does not morally have the right to abdicate his responsibility to govern his life by reasons, and no group of persons or an institution such as the state can take away from him the right and the obligation of being, in this sense, autonomous. Further, I have indicated, but only very sketchily argued for, my own frankly naturalistic position that substantive ethical conclusions must ultimately appeal to man's interests and needs. What remains is to inquire whether autonomy is compatible with political authority. Put another way: the question is whether man does have good reason to obey a political authority.

III

Wolff has very definite views on the nature of authority and of obedience to authority. He defines authority as the right to command, and obedience as compliance with the command of an authority simply because the command has been issued. Insofar as he addresses himself to the question of the way in which an authority acquires its alleged right to command, Wolff considers a version of Max Weber's well-known categorization of ideal

types of authority, according to their kind of legitimacy: traditional, legal–rational, and charismatic.[16] Wolff recognizes, however, that Weber's sources of legitimacy do not establish the
right to command, but rather explain why people come to accept
the claim that someone has the right to command. They offer an
explanation of a fact, not a justification of a moral claim. If
someone has the right to command someone else, this right must
be established by moral argumentation and not by sociological
analysis. Wolff concludes that no such line of moral argumentation can be constructed since the basic obligation of morality is
autonomy, and obedience to authority is a surrender of autonomy.

In order to respond to Wolff we need a further investigation
of the concept of authority than has so far been presented.
Wolff's definition of authority as the right to command, and
correlatively, the right to be obeyed is satisfactory as far as it
goes.[17] But the further question concerning the source of the
right to command must be explored.

Man's fundamental moral obligation is to govern his life by
reasons which receive their specific content from a consideration
of human interests and needs. I shall henceforth refer to this
obligation as the obligation to be humanly reasonable. If obedience to an authority is morally justifiable, then it must be because it is humanly reasonable to obey. Are there then circumstances in which it would be in the human interest and would
serve a human need for a man to do what another man commands? An affirmative answer is possible only if there is a situation in which the man who commands commands what is reasonable, given human interests and needs, and there is a need that he
so command. If what is commanded is not humanly reasonable,
then to obey would be materially wrong, i.e., not in the human
interest. If there were no need that a command be given, then to
obey would be formally wrong, i.e., a surrender of human autonomy. But does a situation, which answers to this general description, and which thus would justify one's obeying another, as a
matter of fact exist? I think so.

It clearly exists in the case of someone, e.g., a philosophy
professor, obeying his doctor's orders. Health is a human need.
The presumption is that the doctor knows better than the philosopher what means will lead to the preservation or restoration of

health. If the doctor does not have such knowledge, then he is simply a quack, and has no authority. There is a need that doctors give commands because philosophy professors cannot reasonably be expected to have as much knowledge about medicine as someone who has made this his profession. The reason the doctor has authority is that what he prescribes is more likely to lead to the desired end, health, and that it is normally impossible, or at least undesirable, for someone to try to achieve expertise in both medicine and philosophy (or, alternatively, that it is unlikely that even someone with adequate expertise, and *a fortiori* the philosopher, will successfully diagnose his own sickness). An authoritative command is thus a command which is reasonable, i.e., one likely to achieve the desired end. Someone is said to be an authority when he is likely to issue reasonable commands. In fact, it is my expectation that the doctor's command is reasonable which justifies my obeying his order. Thus, in submitting to the will of authority, I am not submitting to a heteronomous force, but to my own will insofar as it is rational. Obedience is compliance with a command, not simply because the command has been given, as Wolff maintains, but also because there is reason to think that what is commanded is humanly reasonable.

The example of the doctor and his philosopher–patient can be used to illustrate a further point. The doctor has authority over his patient because the patient has consulted him about his health. The patient desires to be healthy. It is therefore reasonable that he obey his doctor. But consider a philosopher–patient whom years of meditation and brooding have simply made world-weary. Instead of obeying his doctor, he resolves to disobey and prepare for death. Did the philosopher do wrong? A great deal of stage setting would have to be provided—the nature of the disease, e.g., the kind of prescription, the reasons for the philosopher's attitude toward death, his personal commitments, etc.—before we could begin to make moral judgments. But ultimately, I suggest, we would resolve the issue, if resolve it we do, by a consideration of the extent to which human health and specifically the health of this philosopher is an issue of human interest and need. In circumstances, which I leave to my reader's imagination to supply, we might judge that the philosopher had or did not have the right to ignore treatment.

This shows two things: (1) the fact of possible disagreement or uncertainty about a particular moral judgment is perfectly compatible with agreement about the kinds of considerations which are relevant, i.e., the humanly reasonable; (2) at least some human interests and needs—in this case, health—can be subordinate to others.

Where does all this leave us? We have established that there are medical authorities intrinsically constituted as such by the reasonability of their judgments, and that we ought to obey them so long as our commitment to health is not subordinate to and in conflict with some more important good. The question now to be considered is whether there is and ought to be an authority in the political area analogous to an authority in medicine.

IV

The first point to be noted is that if someone is to have the right to command another, this right can possibly be justified only in a limited area, i.e., an area in which it is reasonable that someone else's judgment be followed. Hannah Arendt observed many years ago that liberal writers tend to identify authority with totalitarianism, and that, once this identification is made, they have an easy time showing that authority is morally objectionable.[18] This seems to be Wolff's procedure also, since the kind of political obedience which he attacks is an obedience to whatever is commanded by the state simply because it is commanded. There is no limit to what the state can command. Surely, to obey such a state would be a surrender of autonomy, since there is no rational justification for the command of a state in areas where the individual in his private capacity is able to make his own decisions and pursue his own goals.

However, very few defenders of political authority envision a state with such unlimited authority. It makes sense to defend political authority only if there are genuine human interests and needs which cannot be provided for by the individual himself or cannot be provided for so well by the individual in his private capacity. Thus, the Constitution of the United States does not give to the state unlimited authority, but the authority "to form a more perfect union, establish justice, insure domestic tranquility, provide for the common defence, promote the general welfare, and secure the blessings of liberty to ourselves and our posterity. . . ."[19] These are human interests and needs which cannot be provided for by the individual himself. It is therefore reasonable that there be someone who has the right to make judgments and coordinate efforts and resources for these ends. That is to say, it is morally justifiable that there be a political authority. The right of political authority to command is grounded in social needs inherent in man. It is because men have purposes in common that obeying an authority is a rational way to pursue their ends.

An important conclusion which can be drawn from our analysis is that political authority, like all authority, has an inherent right to be obeyed only when it commands that which is humanly reasonable, and at the same time that which is within its limited sphere of competency.[20] An unreasonable command has no inherent right to be obeyed and ought not to be obeyed unless there are other extraneous reasons to justify complying with the command. For example, it is conceivable that in certain circumstances disobeying an unjust law might bring greater evil on the community than obeying it. A free man obeys the law only because it is just to obey either because of the inherent justice of the law or because of extraneous considerations of the greater good.

One reason for a failure to understand the concept of authority is that it is frequently confused or conflated with the concepts of power and legitimacy.[21] Authority is internally constituted by its reasonability. For this reason Carl Friedrich has argued that authority is primarily and properly a characteristic of a communication or command, and only secondarily of the source of the communication. It is because the communication possesses the "potentiality of reasoned elaboration" that it is worthy of acceptance.[22] Friedrich writes: "He who obeys authority does so because he who orders him to obey appears to have good and sufficient reasons to do so. Authority is not an alternative to reason but is grounded in it."[23]

Legitimacy, on the other hand, is the characteristic of an authority which is *accepted* as having the right to rule. The president of the United States and the members of Congress may not be the best or only political authorities in the United States, but they are legitimate authorities. They are accepted as having the right to rule. It is concerning legitimacy, i.e., the way consent of the governed is achieved, that Weber's kind of sociological analysis is important. But the fact of legitimacy does not by itself guarantee the presence of authority. As Friedrich observes, "What the careful analysis of authority and legitimacy shows is that authority is not 'legitimate power' as is often claimed; for legitimate power may be without authority, a situation which arises in the approach to a revolution." [24]

Power must be distinguished from both authority and legitimacy. It is the capacity to have one's will implemented. Normally authority, simply by virtue of its capacity for reasoned elaboration, possesses a degree of moral power. When political authority achieves legitimacy, a usual concomitant is physical power. But power does not constitute the substance of authority.

It is because Wolff confuses legitimate power with authority that he feels justified in claiming an irreconcilable conflict between authority and moral autonomy. What is correct is that a ruler whose communications do not possess authority, in the sense in which we have explained it, ought not to be obeyed, even though he be fully cloaked with both legitimacy and power. This is the large element of truth in Wolff's position. Wolff regards the concept of a just state as intrinsically contradictory —in the same category as the round square—because he has systematically removed from the concept of legitimate political authority precisely that element which makes it authoritative and deserving our obedience: that is, in Friedrich's terms, its capacity for reasoned elaboration.

V

The arguments in sections II, III, and IV contain the substance of my case in defense of authority and autonomy. In this final section I want to propose several broader metaphysical considerations which are implied by the positions I have taken, and which may serve to illuminate it further.

Wolff's views on political and moral philosophy are ultimately grounded in what I should like to call the liberal individualistic conception of man. It is the view shared by most classical rationalists and empiricists up to and including Kant.

It is common in contemporary existentialists and libertarians. This is the view of man as an isolated individual who comes into contact with his fellows, and only then is called on to reason and deliberate about the commitments and responsibilities which he will assume. Submission to authority is looked upon as in some way a concession which circumstances exact from us; it is something which requires a justification. In political philosophy this liberal individualistic view of man gives rise to versions of contractarianism. In moral philosophy it leads to the ultimate incapacity to show the unreasonability of even the most fanatical behavior. In epistemology it creates the so-called problem of the external world and of other minds.

What is at issue is, of course, the nature of human rationality and understanding. It would be foolish indeed to hope to do justice to this theme in a few brief paragraphs. I do, however, want to sketch what seem to me to be several major considerations relevant to the topic of this paper.[25]

Before an individual is able to arrive at the point at which he can reason and deliberate about the responsible use of his freedom, a whole set of conditions of possibility for such deliberation must be realized. Freedom of choice is possible only if the agent is capable of considering reasons for and against a given course of action. But reasoning itself is an activity which can be done rightly or wrongly. To reason rightly is to act in accord with certain concepts or rules. Concepts and rules, however, are essentially community possessions. They inhere in the institutions and practices which constitute a form of life. The very concept of a concept or rule requires a public criterion which will enable the individual agent to distinguish his understanding the concept or following the rule from his misunderstanding the concept or merely thinking he is following the rule.[26] The individual himself does not decide, by some mythical employment of his sovereign will, what constitutes the concepts or rules which make possible his responsible deliberations about the use of his freedom. A condition of the individual's being a rational agent is that he participate in a community of rationality. Individual rational agents do not come together to produce a community of rationality. The rational community makes possible the very conception of an individual responsible agent. To be a member of a rational community is by that very fact to be subject to an authority—the authority of reason. The members of a rational community drill and train their emerging members in the concepts and rules which will make possible their responsible individual choices. Thus, submission to authority, far from being antithetical to moral autonomy, is a very condition of its possibility.

It has been the burden of this paper to argue that political authority is simply an instantiation of the authority of reason. The ultimate reason man is subject to political authority is simply the fact that he is a rational agent. Although Bernard Lonergan draws conceptual boundaries somewhat different from those which I have elaborated, I believe that my position is in fundamental agreement with his as expressed in a recent article on authority.[27]

Lonergan speaks of man living in two worlds: a world of immediacy revealed in sensation and feeling, and a world "mediated by meaning and motivated by values."[28] The mediated world, if I understand Lonergan correctly, is the world constituted by our concepts, rules, institutions, and practices. "Authority," Lonergan says, "belongs to the community that has a common field of experience, common and complementary ways of understanding, common judgments and common aims. It is the community that is the carrier of a common world mediated by meaning and motivated by values."[29]

I have argued that a claim of authority ought to be obeyed insofar as it expresses that which is humanly reasonable. Of course, what counts as humanly reasonable will vary with historical and cultural situations. What would constitute a responsible response at a particular level of cultural and conceptual differentiation would be irresponsible at another. As Lonergan points out, individuals, authorities, and communities exist in a dialectical relationship which may have as its outcome an authentic or inauthentic world of meaning and value, or, what I have called, a community of rationality. Lonergan writes:

> Meaning and values may be authentic or unauthentic. They are authentic in the measure that cumulatively they are the result of the transcendental precepts, Be attentive, Be intelligent, Be reasonable, Be responsible. They are unauthentic in the measure that they are the product of cumulative inattention, obtuseness, unreasonableness, irresponsibility.[30]

What is wrong with liberal individualism is that it ignores culture, history, tradition, and community. In short, it ignores all that makes it possible for us to be responsible or irresponsible moral agents. There is no wonder that some of its conclusions are unreasonable.

NOTES

1. Robert Paul Wolff, *In Defense of Anarchism* (New York: Harper & Row, 1970).

2. Ibid., p. 4.

3. Ibid., p. 5.

4. Ibid., p. 9.

5. Ibid., p. 12.

6. Ibid., p. 14.

7. Ibid., p. 15.

8. Ibid., p. 71.

9. Ibid., p. 18.

10. Ibid., pp. 21–67.

11. For a fuller discussion of this distinction, see Malcolm Clark, *Perplexity and Knowledge* (The Hague: Nijhoff, 1972), pp. 37ff.

12. Kant sometimes seems to have thought of the categorical imperative as both a necessary and a sufficient condition of moral activity. I agree with Wolff that Kant was not justified in making the stronger claim. Wolff points out that at other times Kant seems to have recognized the categorical imperative as a purely formal principle from which he could not generate substantive moral conclusions. In this mood Kant would appeal to natural obligatory ends to supply content for his ethics. Wolff simply dismisses the notion of obligatory natural ends as nonsense. I shall try to defend a somewhat similar notion later in this paper. See Robert Paul Wolff, *The Autonomy of Reason: A Commentary on Kant's Groundwork of the Metaphysics of Morals* (New York: Harper & Row, 1973), pp. 49ff.

13. See C. D. Broad, *Five Types of Ethical Theory* (New York: Harcourt, Brace, 1930), pp. 116–42.

14. See Wolff, *Autonomy of Reason*, p. 225.

15. Robert O. Johann, "Person, Community, and Moral Commitment," in *Person and Community*, ed. Robert J. Roth, s.j. (New York: Fordham University Press, 1975), pp. 155–75.

16. Wolff, *In Defense of Anarchism*, pp. 6–7. For Weber's analysis, see *Wirtschaft und Gesellschaft* (Tübingen, 1925). Part i of this work has been edited and translated by A. M. Henderson and Talcott Parsons, and published under the title *Theory of Social and Economic Organization* (New York: Oxford University Press, 1947).

17. Wolff, *In Defense of Anarchism*, p. 4.

18. Hannah Arendt, "Authority in the Twentieth Century," *Review of Politics*, 18, No. 4 (October 1956), 405.

19. Preamble to the Constitution of the United States.

20. For a very similar position, see Hanna Pitkin, "Obligation and Consent—I," *American Political Science Review*, 59, No. 4 (December 1965), 990–99; and "Obligation and Consent—II," ibid., 60, No. 1 (March 1966), 39–52.

21. A now classic source of the confusion of authority and power is T. D. Weldon, *The Vocabulary of Politics* (Baltimore: Penguin, 1953), p. 56.

22. Carl J. Friedrich, *Tradition and Authority* (New York: Praeger, 1972), pp. 45–56. Also important is Friedrich's earlier article, "Authority, Reason, and Discretion," in *Nomos. I. Authority*, ed. Friedrich (Cambridge: Harvard University Press, 1958), pp. 35–37.

23. Friedrich, *Tradition and Authority*, p. 55. Friedrich is concerned, of course, as Wolff and I are, with a normative, not a descriptive, notion of "political authority." For a descriptive account which does justice to at least some of the considerations raised in this paper, see C. W. Cassinelli, "Political Authority: Its Exercise and Possession," *Western Political Quarterly*, 14, No. 3 (September 1961), 635–46.

24. Friedrich, *Tradition and Authority*, p. 98.

25. Some of the views which follow have been suggested in somewhat different ways by Wittgenstein, as well as by Stephen Toulmin (*Human Understanding* [Princeton: Princeton University Press, 1972]); Peter Winch, "Authority," *Proceedings of the Aristotelian Society*, Suppl. Vol. 32 (1958), 225–40; Quentin Lauer, s.j., "Authority in the Contemporary World," *Thought*, 45, No. 178 (Autumn 1970), 325–45.

26. This is the main point of Wittgenstein's so-called Private Language Argument. See my article, "Wittgenstein's Use of the Private Language Discussion," *International Philosophical Quarterly*, 14, No. 1 (March 1974), 25–49.

27. Bernard Lonergan, s.j., "Dialectic of Authority," in *Authority*, ed. Frederich J. Adelmann, s.j. (The Hague: Nijhoff, 1974), pp. 24–30.

28. Ibid., p. 25.

29. Ibid., p. 26.

30. Ibid.

7

Social Conflicts
of Freedom and Value

Andrew C. Varga, s.j.

THERE WAS AN EXUBERANT CONFIDENCE around the turn of the century that science and technology would provide limitless progress and an ever-more-perfect world. This optimism has since vanished. Instead, we hear gloomy predictions that we are fast approaching the limits of growth, and that unless we cut back on our expanding consumption of the goods of the earth, catastrophe is inevitable.[1] Although the doomsday prophets are disputed,[2] any would-be optimist must nonetheless face up to some disturbing facts. An increasing scarcity of natural resources and a rapid growth of population could have fatal social and economic consequences.

Of course, careful planning could somewhat change our picture of the future. Adequate steps, however, entail laws and guidelines which must significantly reduce the field of free human activity. My purpose in this brief study is, not to examine in detail any of the proposed plans for controlling world development, but to analyze the value conflicts involved in the designs which are already taking shape. First, I shall offer some general considerations about the threats to freedom of choice which are posed by our technological age. Then I shall briefly analyze the conflicts between freedom and value occurring in both capitalist and socialist economic systems. Next I shall deal with the problems specific to a democratic society—in particular those generated by a constitutional freedom of expression. Finally I shall explore the tensions occasioned by the practice of political freedom and the need for behavior control.

I

Freedom of choice for philosophers as well as for the man in the street means the ability to act in alternative ways or at least the possibility of acting or not acting when the physical conditions for action are present. From the dawn of history, man has been trying to widen the field of free choice, exploring and applying the laws of nature in a variety of ways which increase his options. He began by liberating himself from the power of nature and compelling its forces to serve his purposes. He turned night into daylight, built houses with heat for the winter and, in recent years, cooling devices for the summer. His energy and muscle power are magnified almost infinitely by the machines he has invented. He has even penetrated the hostile environment of outer space. Man today lives in a push-button age, and the range of options facing him is so wide as to be almost frightening. He has succeeded beyond his wildest dreams in broadening the field of free choice.

Yet, at the same time, there are increasing complaints that technology has enslaved man and that the subordination of human beings to machines renders the increase of freedom illusory. The forces organized by modern technology have become so oppressive that men are reduced to the status of mere cogs. They may be distracted by their push-buttons and toys, but in the meantime their real independence and freedom are being choked by the organization of a technological society so complex and ramified that it can be disturbed only at the risk of utter confusion and upheaval. Hence the question: Are we needlessly sacrificing values as the price of "progress"? Is there not an optimum degree of development for a technological system beyond which we cannot go without narrowing the field of free human activity and destroying human values?

In general, we place great value on human freedom. Freedom of choice, or psychological freedom, is the recognized foundation of moral responsibility, and it is a real human value in its exercise. Not every free act, however, is valuable and commendable from the moral point of view. A premeditated murder, for instance, cannot be called a valuable act in spite of the fact that it was committed with full knowledge and freedom. By the same token, when, in the following pages, we analyze the conflicts of freedom and values, we have to keep in mind that not every limitation of freedom is bad. In other words, voluntary compliance with a rational norm will produce value, while unrestricted exercise of freedom may destroy it. But to apply physical or psychological force to human beings and thus curtail their ability to choose freely is dehumanizing because it lessens or destroys moral responsibility. It is logically inferred from this that man has the right to follow the light of his reason. In other words, he has the right of freedom of conscience, and he owes it to himself to live and act accordingly as long as such action is compatible with equal freedom in others. Otherwise he goes against his own best interests.

It is evident, then, that we have to limit our freedom voluntarily in order to assure the achievement of certain values. If every driver insists on the freedom to drive as he pleases, the result is chaos and nobody can drive at all. Industrial society, however, seems to require more than voluntary cooperation; it presses man into a process of production which is broken up into small impersonal and mechanical units. The typical example of this is the assembly line which workers experience as stultifying torture and employers defend as a necessary means if the billions of people of this planet are to be adequately provided with the necessities of life.

Georg Picht, professor of the philosophy of religion at the University of Heidelberg,[3] analyzes with great insight the crisis produced by a constantly growing organization of industry and, indeed, of all aspects of human life. Time has become an impersonal, physical time, alienated from us and hopelessly fragmented. It does not matter who handles the unit of time on the production line; the man handling the unit is replaceable, and the more interchangeable he is, the better for the technology of production. We speak of millions or billions of working hours completely detached from human beings and interchangeable within the industry. Yet time in the life of a person is not interchangeable; it is unique and not repeatable. Every person has a history which evolves between birth and death. His personal historical time cannot be quantified as physical time is quantified in our technological world.

Here, then, is the price of progress. Most of us spend the greater part of our lives on the assembly line of a technological world, and those lives themselves become quantified, stripped of quality and content. Even our "free time" is torn from our personal historical time as we are constantly pressured into consuming what we have produced in our impersonal, physical working time lest we lose our job because of declining demand for the products of our labor. We seem to be caught in a vicious circle and fail to fill our unique and unrepeatable life span with quality and value.

A solution to this conflict of freedom and value is not easy to find. For we simply cannot afford, either in the capitalist or in the socialist camp, to return to a less mechanized and rationalized production system when there is an increasing demand for the necessities of a humane existence by a growing population and a developing world.

The tension between the freedom of the individual and his social obligations stems from his very nature. Man's individual needs and desires are greater than his individual power to satisfy them; they can be fulfilled only by the cooperative effort of society. This fact places obvious limits on individual freedom. In a lifeboat nobody is allowed to jump around; each must follow orders for the sake of everyone's survival. In the common productive effort, too, everyone must pull his weight in an organized way. Modern technological society, however, seems to narrow the field of freedom to such an extent that man becomes the slave of the machines and organizations he has created. In a predominantly agricultural society, organization was less stringent, and man found more fulfillment in his work as he became master, so to speak, of the whole cycle of the life process from beginning to end. The same was true in regard to the less mechanized handicrafts, for a craftsman found personal fulfillment and pride in his work. The complaints of the modern factory worker about the emptiness and monotony of his task are well known. We are also familiar with the various attempts to eliminate the mechanical aspects of work and to make man less subservient to the dictates of the machine. Science and industry were supposed to augment the possibility for the exercise of our freedom of choice, but, although they ensured the physical survival of billions of people, many of these people have become trapped in a treadmill and cannot get out to regain their freedom. The crisis and alienation of technological man is the result, to a great extent, of this conflict of organizational constraint and the yearning for freedom and personal fulfillment.

To get out of this impasse, the Marxist–Leninists promise the final liberation of man in the perfect communist society in which working time is reduced to a minimum and everybody can choose the occupation he finds most satisfying. Organization will lose its dehumanizing character, and even the state will "wither away," giving place to the "self-government" of socially conscious persons. But the difficulty with this and all utopian schemes is that they all end in tyranny as they try to carry out an unrealistic project which has to be imposed upon a nation by force. The promised date of liberation is pushed into the misty future, and what remains of the dream is the never-ending thorny road toward a mirage.

It cannot be realistically suggested that mankind should return to a productive system of handicrafts or a predominantly agricultural economy because division and mechanization of labor is necessary even for a minimal satisfaction of the needs of the large population we have today. During the past century there has been a continuing reduction of working time and an increase of "free time," but man's "liberation" from the bonds of physical and mechanical time by the introduction of faster and more automatic machines is not yet in sight. Although we have to strive to establish the optimum balance between necessary constraint and freedom, the individual as a member of society can never be completely "liberated" from the laws and constraints of social living. The increase of man's freedom should come from within as a person integrates his occupation, even monotonous work, into his own life history. Man can understand and value his own work as a contribution to the life of society in shaping the progress and history of mankind. Beyond his "job," however, every person should realize that he has an individual history and that he is called to build his own personality. Beyond the field of a socially necessary work, a person has a fairly vast area in which to exercise his freedom of choice and direct his actions toward the realization of the good. He can build the "real human" in himself which transcends the narrow confines of a given society and the borders of a material world. Every person experiences, at least occasionally, the pull of the infinite and the attraction of the absolute. Writing his own history through the means of free choices, he can strive toward the realization of the meaning of his own life, achieve an integrated existence, and realize the values he saw in reflecting on the challenge and goal of life.

This is obviously an idealistic presentation, in the sense that a great many people will not reflect on the challenges of human living and will just drift, doing day by day the chores technical society assigns to them. But we should not underestimate the power of rational thinking which every normal human being possesses, nor accept in a fatalistic way the concept that the "masses" will always live life just on the fringes of rationality. There are very few normal human beings who would never ponder about the challenge and purpose of human existence. It is a mission of society, and especially of those who are in charge of the organization of our technical world, to lessen the conflict between human freedom and social living so that men can be masters of their own destinies and can freely write their own individual histories.

Progress and technology, as we have seen in the foregoing analysis, pose several dilemmas. While science in its practical application increases the possibility of different choices—in other words, widens the field of freedom—it frequently ends up placing limitations on freedom as a complex organization asserts its predetermined needs to assure the smooth running of an evergrowing machinery. These dilemmas enter into many spheres of life, and the tension between individual freedom and the requirements of an orderly existence of society produce conflicts of values which often force people into opposing and hostile camps. We have already considered the general aspects of these conflicts. Let us now turn our attention to a few concrete examples.

II

We are used to such terms as "free economic system" (or capitalism) and "planned economy" (or socialism) and are painfully aware of the problems attendant on a free economic system—especially during a recession when millions of persons eager to earn a decent living have no choice but to swell the number of the unemployed. The advocates of socialism are wont to point to the destruction of human values which occurs when the happiness and self-respect of millions of human beings are sacrificed on the altar of free competition while the capitalist system goes through the ups and downs of a business cycle every four to five years. Countless books are written each year praising the advantages of one or the other system and pointing out the shortcomings of its opposite. My point here is not to enter into the technical evaluation of either of the two, but to indicate the antagonism between them which is generated by the presence or absence of freedom.

Unlimited freedom and free competition in the so-called free economic system can exploit the weak and the ignorant and limit the freedom of the masses, with the result that the system subverts its own basic principle of freedom of action for everybody. The free economic order, nevertheless, laid the foundation of mass production, and in many countries it lifted the workers into the middle class. It also enabled large segments of the population to enjoy a style of life which allowed many men and women to enrich their personalities and pursue different goals and values than would otherwise have been possible for them.

The communists, on the other hand, boast that their system has eliminated unemployment and that their centrally planned and directed economy looks after the interests of everyone in a just and equal way. Reality differs from theory, however, and the identifying marks of most communist countries are shortages, low productivity, long lines in front of stores, and shabby products. In addition to this, freedom of movement and expression are so severely curtailed that the value of greater economic security is more than offset by the restrictions imposed on the human spirit.

It would be unfair summarily to condemn both systems in a few sentences when the questions involved are very complex and multifaceted. What I want to point out is the seeming social conflict of economic security and freedom. If one achieves security and full employment through central planning and direction, one necessarily diminishes the field of freedom. Complete freedom, on the other hand, will result in insecurity, constant competitive struggle for one's daily bread, and, frequently, unemployment. The question is whether we can find an equilibrium between these opposing values and achieve the optimum degree of security and freedom. Both sides are often compelled to borrow the other's economic weapons to correct the most evident defects of their respective systems. In free economic systems regulation of the economy and even wage and price controls are not uncommon, while in the socialist camp incentives are provided and some degree of competition allowed in order to stimulate production. Theoretically, the solution would seem to be to rely on the intelligent and social nature of man. We should see to it that the dominant trait of this nature—viz., its capacity for cooperation—is built into man's productive activity and not an antagonistic opposition of partners in the same productive enterprise. All the partners have a common interest in the productive process, and an institutionalized assurance of this common interest could eliminate hostility and achieve, at the same time, a certain degree of freedom. This may sound like an impractical and idealistic statement. Yet, as a matter of fact, many conflicts in this area have been resolved once the litigants turned to the examination of their common interests and were guided by reason and cooperative willingness. Especially good results were achieved when common interests were assured by some institutional arrangement.[4] To be sure, the tension between freedom and human values in the economic field will always be felt. But we can achieve a certain degree of balance between them if we constantly refrain from emphasizing either factor to the detriment of the other in the dynamic and always changing process of productive activity.

III

Ideally, democracy is a system which tries to bring about the highest degree of free cooperation in organizing all the activities which go into a nation's life. It appeals to reason in proposing programs and ideas best suited to fulfill human aspirations with the least restriction on freedom and curtailment of self-determination which is possible under the circumstances. The democratic ideal means talking things out, comparing advantages and disadvantages of opposing ways of action, and letting the majority, presumably the saner part of a nation, decide which way it will go.

Aristotle[5] describes democracy as mob rule, the perversion of polity or constitutional government. What we call democracy or "polity" is a question of definition. Yet Aristotle rightly pointed out the problem inherent in every democracy: namely, the danger that a majority can easily become tyrannical by making it impossible for the wiser to be heard and followed. Recent and past history of democratic regimes in different parts of the world, including the United States, furnish ample proof that the democratic system does not always or infallibly promote and defend the interests of the individual citizen in the best possible way. Slavery, the suppression of the rights of minorities, to mention just two abuses, are painfully present in our memory, and there is no need to dwell upon them.

In order to arrive at the best course of action, one should be able freely and intelligently to compare competing ideas. This, unfortunately, is a very difficult process. Political campaigns are noted, not for the quality of debate, but for their efforts to persuade even at the expense of truth. The American two-party system is frequently praised as one of the best ways of making democracy work. Yet this system makes it very difficult for anyone to get elected to higher office unless he works within the party bureaucracy.

These few reflections are offered, not to criticize or condemn democracy, but only to indicate that the delicate balance of freedom and basic human values is not automatically achieved even within the democratic order which many Americans almost equate with a religious faith. Constant vigilance, prudence, and honesty are necessary to reconcile the interests of all citizens in such a way that human values and freedom are protected and their ever-labile balance is maintained.

IV

Freedom of expression and especially its chief modern application, freedom of the press and of the mass media of communication, are considered to be the best safeguard of freedom and human rights in the political and social life of a nation. It is assumed that knowledge of the truth promotes the most rational conduct in man, and that freedom of expression through the different channels of mass communication assures us of access to that knowledge. It is only natural that authoritarian governments and dictators try to determine the content of the press in

order to control the lives of their subjects. The history of censorship shows how citizens and governments fought for the right to
control the communication of news and even of scientific facts.
Not long after the invention of the printing press, many rulers
and governments correctly came to the conclusion that it would
be a tremendous force in shaping the life of a nation and so they
claimed exclusive rights to grant permission for books to be
printed. In 1556, for instance, the Crown of England granted a
charter to the Stationers' Company which limited printing to
the members of the company and those licensed by it. In ex-
change the company assumed the duty to search out illegal and
undesirable books.[6] Since that time, freedom of the press has
become one of the basic human rights in democratic countries
as constitutional regimes were progressively established.

The basis for the right to freedom of expression is the assumption that this freedom enables a society to be informed of events
in an objective way and to find out the truth in all spheres of
human activity which are relevant to the welfare of the community. Further, this freedom enables individuals to compare
conflicting ideologies in a rational way so that they can adhere
to one or the other, persuaded by reason and not compelled by
force. The sad results of the suppression of freedom of social
communication in communist and authoritarian countries are
well known. Freedom of expression itself can be abused, however, and the defense of this right as unlimited may produce the
opposite of what is intended. The result can be the concealment
of truth and the manipulation of the human intellect by false
arguments and tactics of deception.

Theoretically and ideally, everyone has the right of freedom
of expression, but in the practical order the exercise of this right
(e.g., by publishing a newspaper or operating a radio or television station) presupposes considerable financial means. The
access of the average citizen to these means of social communication is obviously quite limited. Thus a certain "establishment"
of the mass media seems to be a natural and almost necessary
consequence of modern technology. The networks will inevitably
dominate the field, and the more expensive it is to operate independent stations, the more restricted the exercise of freedom of
expression becomes for the man in the street. Also the right of

the citizen to have different sources of information is curtailed. Yet this right is important for him if he is to be able to determine the objectivity of reports and opinions. Since the majority of Americans get their information today from television and radio, it is evident that the power of those who have the privilege of addressing almost the entire nation every night has grown enormously and, in a certain sense, may even exceed the power of the government. Actually the media can and do investigate government operations, and scrutinize the opinions and motives of the president and other officials in press conferences, while they themselves remain immune from cross-examination in their reporting and news analysis. The angry citizen who writes in or is allowed to respond to an editorial at the pleasure, and by the selection, of the network hardly constitutes an exception to this.

Reporters and mass media people like to think of themselves as objective observers dedicated to truth. One does not doubt that many of them try to be objective and have the good intention to serve the public impartially. The question remains whether objectivity is always possible. The fact that most newspaper reporters and organs of the mass media can be classified according to the convictions and ideologies they adhere to, whether they are liberal or conservative or somewhere in between, indicates that they look at events from their particular bias and that their bias shows in their reporting. It may be manifest in the selection of words, in the composition of captions and headlines, in the omission of "insignificant" details, in the emphasis on certain aspects of an event, in the selection of photographs, and in other quiet and almost imperceptible forms of censorship. If we add to this a bias in selecting the sources of news, in the hiring and firing of employees, we can see that objectivity can easily be lost in the shuffle, and the exercise of freedom of expression at odds with the truth and other human values. Considering all this, some political leaders with strong ideological backgrounds can come to the conclusion that the press should be censored in the interest of truth and for the welfare of the nation. But who can assure us that political leaders possess the truth and are immune to bias? History is a clear proof to the contrary. Rulers and politicians are no more infallible and more selfless than the media people, and to entrust the guardianship of truth to them would jeopardize the truth itself, which is so necessary for dignified human living.

The control of the media of communication must not be given to any one group no matter how vigorously it proclaims its dedication to truth and objectivity. Man is a fallible creature in regard to his ability to reach truth and honestly to strive for the good. The conflict of the right of freedom of expression and the right of the public to know the truth can evidently occur even in a democratic country. Although most Americans have a healthy skepticism (according to a Gallup poll, some 75%) concerning the objectivity of the media, this does not prevent them from sitting in front of the television screen every night and absorbing biased interpretations and analyses of events.

It is evidently not easy to work out a system which would achieve a balance of freedom of expression and an assurance of truth and other human values based upon it. It has been suggested that if real freedom of the press exists, i.e., if all the different viewpoints are adequately presented in the media, the public is better informed and people can find truth more easily. The problem is that some groups will never have the financial and political power to have their own publications or to have access to the mass media. Governments could assure a greater diversification of the media, but the practical difficulties are not negligible.[7] It is not our purpose in this brief study to recommend practical and concrete solutions to this very complex question. Nevertheless, a general principle could be enunciated: namely, that every organ in society should be responsible to the people in some systematic way. The president and the government are responsible to the people through elections and in other manners. The media, however, unless they are involved in libel or some other evident violation of the law, are exempt from all organized social control. Citizens should be given the possibility of engaging in an open dialogue with the media through selected representatives of various backgrounds, and of challenging the reporting and self-assured analysis of the media people.

It seems clear that we are faced in this case with a serious and potentially dangerous conflict of freedom and human values. Its resolution will test the good will, honesty, and intelligence of all involved.

V

The terms psychosurgery and behavior control appear on the pages of daily papers with an increasing frequency. This can be taken as a sign of interest on the part of the public in the experiments of behavior modification carried out in laboratories and institutions. With a rapidly rising crime rate and the bizarre behavior of many young, and not so young, persons of the drug culture, the professional protester and dissenter, the thought naturally comes to many minds that science should do something to bring people back to "normalcy." Popular and serious literature abounds in this field.[8] The techniques of brain manipulation cannot be described here in any detail. Some of the instruments were developed by José M. R. Delgado of Yale University. They consist basically of assemblies of very fine wires which are introduced into the skull through small openings and transmit electrical stimulation. They can then be hooked up with a small radio receiver and transmitter called a "stimoceiver."[9] In other experiments, drugs are used to effect the modification of behavior. Or psychological principles are applied, such as rewarding a specified good behavior. START (Special Treatment and Rehabilitation Training), a federal project in Missouri (recently discontinued) for troublesome inmates, is only one example of the many experiments aimed at making "abnormal" persons over into "normal" ones.

There is an evident tension here between the demands of society for a socially acceptable behavior and the freedom of the troublesome or abnormal person. Several questions have to be answered in order to find a satisfactory solution to this conflict. Is the troublesome man or criminal a free agent, or does he act under compulsion and consequently without freedom and responsibility? Is deviation from the generally accepted norm of behavior a sign of abnormality? How much abnormal behavior can be tolerated in a society without undermining the order necessary for the functioning of society? Do the techniques of behavior control restore the use of freedom when the abnormal behavior is due to psychological compulsion, or do these treatments reduce a human being to an automaton which, as a result of the treatment, is programed to fit into the huge machinery of society? Did he become more of a human being as his "sociability" was increased or did he become "dehumanized" because his freedom was reduced to conditioned reflexes? All these questions point to ethical problems and to potential dangers to a free society. Will these individuals gain self-control and self-possession through these techniques? Are they really liberated, or are they instead forced into conformity? Are they rebuilt into free human beings or only made over into manageable means for certain goals of society?

Delgado, differing with B. F. Skinner, insists that these techniques should be used to increase one's freedom. A person "should be trained and encouraged to use the given building blocks of his personality in some original way according to the unique combination of circumstances which constitute his personal identity." [10] Critics of the projects and experiments to alter behavior admit the good will of many scientists. Nevertheless, they are concerned about the inherent dangers to human freedom and to basic human values upon which the life of an orderly society is based. Their questioning prompted some legislatures to enact laws for the protection of human values. Oregon was the first to enact a law in 1973 "to provide the strictest possible control over the advocacy and practice of operations specifically aimed at permanently altering behavior." [11] The Department of Health, Education and Welfare issued detailed rules and regulations in 1974 for "the protection of human subjects." In 1974 Congress established a "National Commission for the Protection of Human Subjects of Biomedical and Behavioral Research." The Commission has a two-year mandate to recommend policy to the Secretary of the Department of HEW and to Congress.[12]

As reports of chemical straitjackets and of overdoses of tranquillizers and the other drugs used in mental institutions to make patients "behave" instead of curing them increases, the demands for the control of these practices and for the safeguarding of the rights of mental patients are becoming more pronounced and better argued. Suggestions for legislation in this regard seem to go in the right direction. Most of the proposals point out the social conflicts of human values and individual freedom. In the complex web of these interrelationships and confrontations, laws are necessary and useful, but they can give only general directives to resolve the contradictions because every case is unique and involves conflicting values in various degrees. The persons involved in treating these cases will have to judge how the optimum degree of an individual's liberation from compulsive forces and his integration into the fabric and cooperative work of society can be achieved.

The examples of social conflict of freedom and values discussed in the previous pages point to two dynamic tendencies in man: his assertion of freedom on the one hand, and his existential need for social cooperation on the other. These two forces sometimes come into such a direct collision that one may get the impression that either freedom or some important value is certain to become a casualty. Yet they must be integrated. For freedom of choice should not be conceived as if it means an equal potency for value or lack of value, or as if freedom is lessened when a person chooses good over evil. Freedom of choice is a means for good actions by which man builds his humanity. Freely choosing the good, even the socially necessary good, is not a curtailment of freedom but its fulfillment. Freedom of choice does not mean remaining undetermined forever; it means, rather, the ability to decide and act freely. It follows that once an alternative has been chosen, the purpose of freedom has been achieved in this particular case. Nevertheless, the tension between society and the individual remains real, for social and individual interests may seemingly or even really conflict with each other. There is no magic formula which would solve this tension once and for all. Man grows and builds his humanity by daily facing these tensions and trying to achieve a delicate balance between opposing values. The dynamism of these counteracting forces is constantly changing with changing circumstances, but the opposition is ultimately not so deep as it first appears, since man is basically a social being and his personality can be fulfilled only by actions which strengthen society, and through society, the individual himself. We have to keep in mind in this regard that society is not a substance which can exist in itself; it exists only in its members, who are rational substances, i.e., persons, and subsist in themselves. On the other hand, it belongs to the essential characteristics of persons that they are social beings and consequently can be fulfilled, even in their individuality, only through social cooperation. Thus the conflict of society and individual, freedom and value, can be solved by the free acts of persons who prudently choose genuine values which promote their personal growth within the framework of society.

NOTES

1. On the controversy aroused by the first report to the Club of Rome, see *The Limits to Growth*, edd. Donella H. Meadows et al. (New York: Universe, 1972); for an opposing view, see *Models of Doom*, edd. H. S. D. Cole et al. (New York: Universe, 1973).

2. See John Maddox, *The Doomsday Syndrome* (New York: McGraw-Hill, 1973).

3. Georg Picht, "Unter dem Diktat der physikalischen Zeit," *Evangelische Kommentare*, 8, No. 2 (February 1975), 75–77.

4. The *Mitbestimmungsrecht* (Right of Co-determination) in West Germany, for example.

5. Aristotle, *Politics* iii.7.

6. Harry Street, *Freedom, the Individual and the Law* (Harmondsworth: Penguin, 1963), p. 99.

7. Robert Cirino, *Power to Persuade* (New York: Bantam, 1974), p. 215.

8. *L'Homme manipulé*, ed. Charles Robert (Strasbourg: Cerdic Publications, 1974); Erwin Lausch, *Manipulation* (Glasgow: Fontana/Collins, 1975); Gerald Leach, *The Biocrats* (New York: McGraw-Hill, 1970), to cite but a few.

9. José M. R. Delgado, "Brain Manipulation: Psychocivilized Direction of Behavior," *The Humanist*, 32, No. 2 (March–April 1972), 11.

10. Ibid., 15.

11. *Oregon Laws* (1973), Chapter 616.

12. *Federal Register* (May 30, 1974), pp. 18914–20.

8

Duty and Reason
in Thomistic Social Ethics

GERALD A. McCOOL, s.j.

THE EPISTEMOLOGICAL AND METAPHYSICAL GROUNDING of duty and reason in general ethics and the interrelation of these two notions in social ethics are classical problems which remain live issues today. Competing schools of contemporary philosophy, notably analytic philosophy and phenomenology, have taken diverse approaches to them and come up with quite different solutions. Much discussion about these topics has gone on among the analysts and phenomenologists themselves, and a good deal of debate about them has been carried on between representatives of these competing orientations. Indeed discussion about the theoretical grounding of duty and reason and debate about the satisfactoriness of theories concerning their interrelationship have influenced the internal development of analytic and phenomenological social ethics. This is hardly news, of course, to American philosophers. What would be news to most of them, however, is that this evolution in the philosophy of duty and reason has any relation to Thomism. If American ethicians think of Thomism at all, they assume that the philosophy of duty and reason in present-day Thomistic social ethics remains what it was in the social ethics of Jacques Maritain. They take it for granted that the epistemology and philosophy of man which support present-day Thomistic social ethics are still the epistemology and philosophy of man whose classical expression is found in Maritain's *The Degrees of Knowledge*.[1]

This is not the case, however. A remarkable evolution in epistemology and philosophy of man has been going on in the transcendental Thomism for which Maritain never had much sympathy. This evolution has produced a new social ethics which, while remaining faithful to the natural law tradition, has become much more flexible and sophisticated than the conventional Thomistic social ethics.

The larger philosophical community in the United States has remained unaware of this evolution for two main reasons. First, its two leading representatives, Karl Rahner and Bernard J. F. Lonergan, although very competent philosophers, work in a theological context and their works are read by theologians rather than philosophers. Secondly, very little has appeared in print about the relation of their ethics to analytical ethics.

The present essay is a preliminary step toward bridging this communications gap. It will endeavor to acquaint philosophers belonging to other traditions with the possibilities of the new transcendental Thomistic approach to social ethics by focusing on two pivotal notions of duty and reason. The essay will first discuss the epistemological and metaphysical framework in which its philosophy of duty and reason is inserted. It will then attempt to show how, within this framework, a basically Thomistic understanding of these two notions is an important element in contemporary transcendental Thomism's flexible, open, and evolving social ethics. Finally, it will endeavor to show how, in practice, a theological context can still be a fruitful source for ethical insights, although, as always, the problems involved in the translation of these insights into a strictly philosophical context can be difficult. Some of these problems will be touched on in the course of this essay. Unfortunately, an adequate discussion of them—which would have to consider the anticipated objections of analytic ethicians—exceeds the limits of an introductory exposition.

THE NEW PHILOSOPHICAL FRAMEWORK:
MAN'S QUESTION ABOUT GOD

As transcendental Thomists, Rahner and Lonergan ground their metaphysics of *esse* by transcendental reflection on the *a priori* conditions of possibility for the human subject's acts of knowledge and love. According to both, the condition of possibility for man's conceptual knowledge and for his acts of free choice is the human subject's conscious, though implicit, awareness of Infinite Being as the goal of his intellectual and volitional dynamism. The goal of man's spiritual striving is the Infinite Perfection of Being, pure *esse*. As pure *esse*, God must be Spirit, the Pure Act of Knowledge and Love. The Infinite Spirit is the unitary source of both the dynamic intelligibility of nature and the dynamic intelligence of man. Furthermore, as the infinite, self-possessing identity of being, intelligibility, and goodness, God is a person.[2]

At first there seems little new in this approach to God. It reads like a rehearsal of the transcendental Thomist natural theology whose origin goes back to Joseph Maréchal's *Le Point de départ de la métaphysique*.[3] Many years ago Joseph de Fever's *La Preuve réelle de Dieu*[4] and, more recently, Henri Bouillard's *The Knowledge of God*[5] acquainted European and American Thomists with this type of natural theology; and, although Gilsonian and Maritainian Thomists have never taken kindly to it, a generation of American undergraduates has become familiar with its brief and lucid exposition in Joseph Donceel's *Natural Theology*.[6] Rahner and Lonergan, however, have inserted this basically Maréchalian natural theology into a new context; and, in this new context, the possibilities for its employment in philosophical ethics have become more apparent.

Knowledge, expressed in the judgment, is the answer to a prior question. If man never asks a question, he will never know. The dynamism of the human spirit therefore is a dynamism which first asks and then answers questions. But, as Heidegger and Gadamer have shown us, there is no such thing in man's concrete experience as a presuppositionless question. Questions can be raised and answered only against the background of an horizon. Sometimes a shift of horizon must take place before a question can even be raised intelligently. Questions arise in a definite world of meaning. If they are asked on a level of any depth, they are provoked by the questioner's acquired and inherited experience and by the vital concern aroused by conflict between that experience and his ongoing encounter with the world of daily life. A real question about God, a question which arises on the level of human concern, is far from being a logical exercise for man's discursive reason. On the contrary, a real question about God is the thematization of the human subject's concrete response, cognitive and affective, to the world which he faces and to the horizon against which that world appears.

Rahner equates the question of God with the question of Being.

It follows that for Rahner the question about God is unavoidable, at least on the implicit level of human action.[7] Every man must choose himself in action through the lived implicit choice of his fundamental attitude toward the world of fact and value;[8] and an answer to the question about Being, the ground of meaning and value, enters implicitly into the intentionality of any decisive choice of attitude toward that world. Man's real question about Being, moreover, transcends the realm of discursive logic.[9] It calls into question the intelligibility which discursive intelligence presupposes in its proofs. Thus the philosopher who refuses to count any data as evidence unless they are the objective type of data which yield themselves to linguistic analysis and to the logical operations of scientific method, has profoundly misunderstood the nature of man's question about Being. We should not be surprised that he finds himself incapable of answering it.

The question about Being and God confronts man in the full intentionality of the great human experiences in which he responds to his world both cognitively and affectively. These experiences—the experience of love, responsible choice, deep joy, loneliness, desolation, and death, for example—are experiences of the whole man.[10] The knowledge contained in the whole man's concrete response to their challenge is not the abstract objective knowledge of the detached pure observer. It is the personal knowledge of the concrete human agent and, as such, its ability to grasp reality is profoundly influenced by the affective attitude which the knower adopts to the known in his concrete action. Man's implicit answer to the question of God and Being is given in his concrete response to his world of fact and value. The right answer to that question becomes explicit when the human knower clearly understands that the drive of his human spirit, which provokes his personal questions about meaning and value and moves him to choose himself in his attitude toward the world, would be unintelligible unless its goal were the existent Infinite Act of Being.

In his recent book *Philosophy of God and Theology*, Bernard Lonergan argues that man's real question about God arises on all the levels of his conscious dynamism.[11] The first is the level of intelligence. On this level the human knower's effort to grasp the meaning of a sense datum provokes the question "What is it?" The dynamic drive of human intelligence to understand, which provoked that question, comes to rest in the act of insight which grasps the universal intelligibility immanent in the concrete sense datum. Once it is grasped in the act of insight, this universal intelligibility can be consciously formulated—with varying degrees of adequacy—in a concept which, we may remark in passing, is both revisable and intrinsically conditioned by its relation to other concepts in its scientific, historical, or cultural conceptual framework. Man's reflection on the movement of his own mind will show him that the question "What is it?" is provoked by the drive of the intellect to understand. But is man's drive to understand any more than an urge for subjective satisfaction? Or is it a drive whose goal is an objective intelligibility? If the latter be the case, then the sensible world which confronts the human intellect on the level of intelligence must itself be intrinsically intelligible. But does not an intelligible world require an intelligible ground? Again, since human intelligence itself requires a ground, must not the world's ground be intelligible intelligence? But to ask the question about the intelligent ground of the world's intelligibility is to ask the question about God.

The second level of understanding is the level of reflection, the level of the judgment, on which the human knower asks the question "Is it so?" The knower can give an affirmative or negative answer to this question only if his experience verifies that all the conditions required to justify his answer have been fulfilled. Verification is required on the level of reflection because the objects of our sensible universe are not absolutely unconditioned necessary beings. They are contingent; and, being contingent, they are no more than virtually unconditioned realities. In other words, they are beings which exist when the conditions required for their existence have been in fact fulfilled. But is not the existence of an absolutely necessary being required to account for the existence of beings whose own existence is conditioned? And, so, the question about God recurs on the level of reflection.

The third level of human understanding is the level of deliberation, the level on which the conscious human agent deliberates about his choices. To deliberate, however, is to ask whether a contemplated course of action is really worth while. But does "worth while" mean anything more than useful or subjectively satisfying? Or does the human good toward which man strives demand that there be—especially on the moral level—genuine objective values? Is the realm of moral values purely of man's making? Did it begin with the human race? If so, the universe is intrinsically amoral, and man's moral strivings seem doomed to failure. But if, on the contrary, the universe is basically moral, must not its necessarily existent intelligent ground also be a highly moral being? Once again the question about God recurs, this time on the level of deliberation.

MAN'S EXPERIENCE OF TRUTH AND VALUE

A number of points should be observed about the insertion of the Maréchalian approach to God into the new context of man's unavoidable concrete question about God and Being. In its new setting the Maréchalian proof takes the form of a philosophical reflection on the whole dynamism of man's spiritual action. This dynamism is an indivisible conscious unit. It is set in motion by the knower's encounter with sense data prior to conceptualization and judgment. Its conscious drive carries it through the judgment to the free decision in the realm of value. The evidence on which the proof rests, therefore, is not found on the level of the concept. Neither is it found on the level of discursive reasoning. The intelligibility of man's total conscious dynamism can be grasped only on the level of higher reason (*intellectus, Vernunft*) since it transcends and grounds the intelligibility of man's lower discursive reason (*ratio, Verstand*). When it is grasped and thematized, the intelligibility of the human spirit reveals that its dynamism is a unitary conscious movement toward man's human good.[12] This dynamic appetite precedes concepts and judgments, and drives beyond them. Since the movement of man's spirit is a tendency toward a single goal, man's personal knowledge of his world is conditioned by the intentionality of his affective attitude toward it. His conscious choice of attitude toward the realm of values vitally affects his ability to make true judgments about reality. Furthermore, his acts of knowledge can occur only in the unified world determined by the horizon toward which his spirit's intentionality is directed. In a unified world, individual judgments are conditioned by the conceptual frameworks into which they must be inserted.[13] Nevertheless, unless it is impeded by the interference of man's other drives, the drive of the human intelligence to understand calls conceptual frameworks into question and leads to their eventual revision.[14] But in fact the concrete knower's continuing drive to understand may be impeded in its free unfolding by his stand to the realm of values.[15]

In other words, the experience in which Rahner and Lonergan locate man's real question about God is the socially and historically conditioned experience of the concrete man. Judgments of fact and value are intertwined with free decisions in this concrete experience and influence each other in its constitution. Concrete experience is not the detached observation of the impersonal observer. It is rich personal knowledge. In personal knowledge the unitary dynamism of the human spirit moves each individual man to respond to the "is" of the virtually unconditioned through the conceptual judgments of his discursive intelligence. At the same time it urges him to commit himself freely to an unremitting effort to understand, because understanding is "really worth while." Understanding is a genuine value, a good which man "ought" to pursue.

Thus the real question about God, which the reflective human knower finds as a "given" in his concrete experience, is the lived question about the ground of the intelligibility and value which man discovers as an undeniable prior "given" in his own experience. It is a lived question whose undeniable presence in man's experience would be unintelligible unless man already possessed —on the level of *intellectus* or *Vernunft*—an implicit awareness of truth and value and of their ground in the personal God. Man's discovery of God is linked to his discovery of a grounded "ought" which rules his conduct, an "ought" which tells him to "act intelligently" because intelligent action is a value which it is his duty to pursue.

Intelligent inquiry may lead a man to a profound moral conversion and to a corresponding shift in the horizon against which his world appears. Or it may lead him to the act of insight which gives rise to a new conceptual framework in which concrete instances of the "really worth while" can be better understood and more accurately evaluated. Man's encounter with God occurs in the context of his unitary response to the world of fact and value.[16] The question of God arises in the lived process of re-

sponsible inquiry which the interplay of duty and reason keeps
in constant motion.

THE MORAL "OUGHT":
A RESPONSE TO THE LOVING GOD

Transcendental reflection upon man's real question about God
lays the groundwork for an ethics based on man's relationship
to God as the creative source of intelligibility and value. Rahner
calls God Infinite Spirit.[17] Lonergan calls him the Pure Act of
Insight.[18] Both speak of God as the Infinite Identity of Being
and Knowledge from whom finite intelligence and intelligibility proceed. If God, the world's creator, is the infinite unity of
being and knowledge, the world must proceed from God by an
intelligible procession and not through the blind contingency of
matter. The human knower's awareness of his own contingence
and finitude tells him that, just as he must participate in God's
intelligence in order to know, the finite beings of his objective
knowledge must participate in God's intelligibility in order to
be knowable. The contingent knower also understands that finite
reality is not only caused but freely caused. No matter how great
a finite world may be, a greater finite world remains conceivable.
For, between any finite reality and the Infinite Identity of Being
and Knowledge, the gap is always limitless. There is no intelligible necessity, therefore, why our concrete world, with its dynamic order of being and value, should have proceeded from
God rather than any other of the countless contingent worlds
which were also possible. Our world, with its dynamic intelligible order, has proceeded from God by the only intelligible procession compatible with its contingence. It has proceeded from
God as the term of his loving act of divine free choice.[19]

Thus, as Thomas saw in his Fifth Way, the dynamic intelligibility of our physical and social world is grounded in God's free
act of continuous creation. And, if this be so, man's exigence for
intelligibility, without which no science or philosophy is possible, terminates in an encounter with an act of personal freedom.
Man's drive to know opens out into the personal relationship
with God which philosophers call religious experience.[20] Response to the intelligible order of truth and value turns out to be
an implicit response to God's loving will. Once that is under-

stood, man can see more clearly the transcendent ground for the link between reason and duty which he has discovered in his own experience. Value is not founded in human utility. Morality is not grounded in a purely aesthetic response to the intelligible beauty of the universe. Morality rests upon true *authority*, the specifically moral *ought*, on the obedience which the free finite person owes to the infinite personal source of finite truth and value. Thus, in contemporary transcendental Thomism, the free knower's fundamental experience of God turns out to be a personal encounter with the personal God of the moral law. Just as there is no problem of the bridge between intramental and extramental reality in its epistemology, there is no problem of the bridge between scientific and normative intelligibility, between the "is" and the "ought," in its ethics.

THE INTERPLAY OF DUTY AND REASON IN GROUNDING SOCIAL ETHICS

In this way transcendental reflection on the human knower's dynamism can provide the epistemological and metaphysical grounding for the basic claims of a natural law morality.[21] The order of truth and value in our contingent world is grounded in God's eternal intellect and will. The exigency for truth, goodness, and beauty in man's spiritual dynamism will not be satisfied until he reaches his truly human fulfillment through submission to the intelligible order of thought and conduct grounded in the holy will of God. God's will manifests itself in the intelligible order of the universe which man's reason can discover. God's personal presence in the human spirit is the source for the absolute demand that the intelligible order of the world be respected in man's free choices. The good (which is the intelligible) must be done. The exact nature of the good, which it is man's duty to accomplish by his action, will reveal itself to his human reason if he honestly and carefully examines the concrete complexus of relations which constitute the material, social, and historical order of his world.

Karl Rahner claims that human reason can discover a number of these relations which are based on man's unrevisable structure as a free knower in the world. Since man is a discursive knower, whose knowledge begins with sense experience, he is not a Platonic spirit. He is spirit in matter, part of the material world, a member of the human race. He is *homo faber*, the intelligent being who molds the earth whose evolution has produced him. He is a sexual, familial being, dependent on his fellow men for his ability to grow, to work the earth, to develop himself socially and culturally.[22] Man's relations to his world, productive, economic, social, and cultural in their nature, carry with them a diverse set of structured relations to his fellow men. An incarnate, social, historical knower can neither work the earth nor fulfill his spiritual exigencies if he remains alone. By the very demands of his being, man is inserted into a network of ordered social units.

His very intelligence which compels man to prefer his own freedom to the material determinism of the biological order compels him to recognize that neither his own freedom nor the freedom of his fellow men can be exercised or developed in an atmosphere of anarchic individuality. Reflecting on the interplay of reason and duty in human experience, Lonergan discovered that "act attentively" and "act reasonably," the laws of the human spirit on the levels of intelligence and reflection, develop into "act responsibly," the law of the human spirit on the level of deliberation.[23] When these two maxims are applied to the social level, they lead to the specific maxim of reason and duty: "Social units must be formed." And since these units are formed to give human action the intelligent direction of which the isolated individual is incapable, moral reason concludes that they must have, in the measure to which intelligent direction requires it, the moral force which is called authority. And if they are not to be futile—and therefore unintelligible—their authority must be vested—again to the extent that it is necessary—with the power of social compulsion which moralists call sanction.

FREEDOM AND SOCIAL AUTHORITY

Transcendental reflection on the interplay of duty and reason in man's concrete experience can establish, in a formal way, the need for a number of societies, each of which will possess, within limits which may not be exceeded, some sort of authority and sanction. Admittedly, an *a priori* reflection on knowledge and volition cannot specify the nature of these societies or define their authority as fully as older natural law ethicians would like. Nevertheless, it can ground a number of significant propositions about them.

Since God is the source and goal of our contingent world, man's free response to God through his intentional stance to the world is man's highest human good. Consequently, no finite reality within the world, whether it be the economic good of *homo faber* or the social good of any national or ethnic grouping, can be put in the place of God as the supreme goal of human striving.[24] For when a finite good is substituted for God as the final goal of human striving, a lived contradiction is set up within the will which dooms it to ultimate frustration. This radical frustration of the human spirit's drive to its proper human good is the inevitable consequence of the false goal which our contemporary ideologies propose to human action. That is the reason for their fundamental immorality.[25] Governments which justify their existence on the basis of these social and political ideologies subvert their own authority because they substitute a finite good for God as the goal of human action, and thus usurp the place of the personal God in whom social and political authority is grounded.

Since the ultimate goal of the spiritual dynamism which unfolds through the interplay of duty and reason is man's free encounter with God, man's growth in intelligible freedom is a precious good. The greater man's effective freedom, the greater his capacity for moral action.[26] The greater man's capacity for moral action, the greater his capacity for a truly personal response to God. Therefore, individual and political freedom may not be sacrificed in favor of lesser goods, such as social order, economic stability (especially for a limited group), or the dominance of a political party or social class. Specific limitations of these freedoms must be justified on the basis of the protection, or more effective promotion, of freedom.[27] Furthermore, there are many subsocieties in our complex social order whose rights and responsibilities must be carefully considered and properly respected. Larger groupings must be able to present convincing reasons to justify their right to assume the functions of smaller social groups. The duty incumbent upon political leaders to respect human freedom requires them to inquire carefully into the limits of their authority to direct the activities of groups and individuals to the common good. They may not arbitrarily extinguish the freedom of individuals and subsocieties to direct their own affairs in the name of political or social ideologies or in the interest of social engineering whose goal is economic or administrative efficiency rather than a growth in human freedom.

CIVIL SOCIETY, THE FAMILY, AND SUBSOCIETIES

This formal deduction of the nature and extent of social authority, valuable as it is as a guide to moral reason in an age of imperiled freedom, remains quite abstract. The further determination of the precise nature of the many societies which constitute the social order of our concrete historical world requires an empirical investigation of man's place in its mutable, evolving, culturally conditioned structures. Contemporary transcendental Thomism is very insistent on this point, and it is much more tentative than traditional Thomism in its concrete application of natural law principles to contemporary societies. Both Rahner and Lonergan are convinced that the role of reason in social ethics cannot be restricted to its transcendental reflection on the dynamism of the human spirit. If modern man is to acquit himself of his duty to act reasonably and responsibly, his moral reasoning must take account of the empirical data derived from history and the natural and social sciences. Nonetheless, moral reason should not undervalue the practical importance of the general principles which flow from the unrevisable structure of an incarnate spirit.

The bisexual nature of the human knower and the value of the human person can still ground the permanent and exclusive character of the marriage commitment. Man's exigency for personal love, and its link, through marriage and generation, to individual incarnation, ground the sanctity of the family as a distinctive social unit. The family's interpersonal relationships are structured by the "I–Thou" intentionality whose term is the individual in his uniqueness. Larger social units are structured by the "I–It" intentionality. A discursive knower cannot deal with large areas of reality unless he subsumes them under the universal categories of his objective knowledge. Civil society, therefore, must operate under the intelligibility of universal laws. It can deal with its subjects intelligently only to the extent to which they fall under the impersonal universals of its legal system, its economics, and its social sciences. Inevitably, then, civil authority must be impersonal. It must be exercised under the abstract laws of judicial equality. "No individual is above the law." Civil society's approach to the citizen cannot be structured by the personal knowledge, the love, and the flexibility with which the head of a family authoritatively directs its members toward their individual and common good.

Thus, prior to any detailed inquiry into the structures of our contemporary society, moral reason can establish through its transcendental reflection on human knowledge and love that there is a fundamental difference between the family and the larger units of civil society. The social bond which unites its citizens within the state is essentially different from the social bond which unites the members of a family. Parents' knowledge of the children whose activity they guide differs essentially from the civil functionary's impersonal knowledge of the citizens whose activity he directs to the common good. If these differences are blurred, the members of familial and civil society can no longer be properly directed by intelligence and love to their individual and common good. Therefore the basic moral maxims "act reasonably and act responsibly" impose on the heads of families and on civil rulers the duty not to blur them. Displacement of the family by the state's bureaucracy in the direction of those areas of life in which personal relations between individuals are most important—such as education, marital relations, family planning, life-and-death decisions affecting the old and the incurably ill—is an intolerable invasion of the freedom and authority of familial society for which the state's own authority gives it no moral warrant.

Nevertheless, although this general scheme of family–state relations is of great practical value, it does not suffice to settle a number of important specific issues in contemporary social ethics. What is the real nature of familial authority today? How does it affect the relations between husband and wife in our contemporary industrial society? How does it affect relations between parents and children in the urban atomic family? How much of the traditional natural law philosophy about parental authority must now be discarded as the outmoded product of a culture and society which modern man has outgrown? How can

we specify more precisely the relationship which should exist
today between the family, subordinate social and economic groupings, and the national government? What is the proper relationship between national governments and world government? Does
the plight of the third world, the exploitation of the earth's resources by vast multinational corporations, and the peril to our
existence by the proliferation of nuclear armaments indicate that
society's need for peace, prosperity, and orderly development
can now be met only by an international government endowed
with true authority? In other words, has the establishment of a
world republic now become a demand of the natural law?

DUTY AND REASON IN AN EVOLVING "WORLD OF MEANING": NORMS FOR JUDGING EMPIRICAL DATA

These specific issues are not easy to handle. Indeed the difficulty
which modern society puts in the way of their reasonable and
responsible solution threatens the ordinary man's ability to take
a personal stand in relation to vital public issues. The nature,
structure, and extent of the social authority which the members
of a society have a corresponding duty to obey are much more
historically conditioned and mutable than the older Thomistic
ethicians thought. Our modern social structures are the product
of history and culture, not just of nature. Our technical society
has become increasingly aware of its own ability to change the
pattern of nature and to alter radically the structure of human
relations by its own technical planning. Widespread awareness
of this power has become in itself a revolutionary force in social
thinking. Ecologists are deeply troubled by the promise and
threat contained in society's ability to change nature by technical
manipulation. Medical techniques helped to create the population explosion. Now these same techniques have posed the moral
problem of a conflict between individual freedom and govern-
mental responsibility in limiting the population of over-crowded
countries.

The calculated use of opinion-making techniques by pressure
groups actively concerned with abortion, homosexuality, and
premarital sex have shown by their success the remarkable
power which organized groups now possess to change long-held,
deep-seated moral attitudes in the general population through

scientific psychological manipulation. Added to this psychological threat to the citizen's ability to determine his own moral attitudes freely through the use of his own moral reason is the more frightening threat which biological manipulation poses to the continuance of a free society. To a limited extent at least, society is now able to produce a new race of men through the techniques of breeding and conditioning. A society's ruling class can breed a new generation of citizens whose programed drives and preplanned responses are more suited to their rulers' purposes than the drives and responses of the present generation.[28]

The basic moral axioms "act reasonably and act responsibly" impose on modern man the duty to face up to the problems of our modern technical society which are posing a serious threat to human freedom. To abstain from action is to yield the field to the forces of irrationality and to the tyranny of power. Passive refusal to act is not the response demanded by the axiom "act responsibly." On the other hand, an unreflective response to a complicated situation is not the proper response to the axiom "act reasonably." Contemporary transcendental Thomists agree with the traditional Thomistic position that the citizens of our modern democracies have a duty to seek a solution to the grave moral problems created by our technical society. Finding a solution to them through an empirical inquiry into its complex social structures, however, presents an enormous challenge to moral reason. Whether traditional Thomism could rise to it is a good question. Transcendental Thomism, however, can provide moral reason with a much more sophisticated epistemology than traditional Thomism possessed. And, although it is much more modest about the extent and the certitude of its conclusions than the traditional Thomistic deductive ethics, its capacity to establish norms by which the structures of an evolving society can be evaluated may turn out to be one of its more useful contributions to contemporary social ethics.

In opposition to traditional Thomism, transcendental Thomism puts great stress on the point that moral judgments in the area of social ethics must be made with full awareness of the culturally conditioned character of our social structures. Transcendental Thomists believe, however, that, when the implications of Lonergan's epistemology are developed further and are systematically applied in social ethics, moral reason will be able to make normative judgments about evolving and historically conditioned societies. Lonergan's celebrated distinction between the acts of insight and its conscious conceptualization led to his equally celebrated discovery of the higher viewpoint, e.g., the intellectual move from arithmetic to geometry. The higher viewpoint is the discovery of a new science, a new conceptual framework, a distinct area of discourse. Although the act of insight provides an intelligible connection between the lower and the higher viewpoint, there is no rational, conceptual connection between the two which can be linked into the chain of a logical deduction.

In his later works Lonergan has made much of the fact that man's judgments must be inserted into diverse cultural as well as diverse scientific conceptual frameworks.[29] Each of these diverse historico-cultural conceptual frameworks is a distinct "world of meaning" determined by the particular horizon toward which the human knower's intentionality is directed. Each "world of meaning" is culturally conditioned. Each changes with the historical shifts in the human knower's conscious intentionality.[30] Every historical "world of meaning" is a world of constituted relationships; and in each the number and nature of the societies which make up its dynamic social order can vary. History and social anthropology have shown that there can be vast differences in the nature of the family, the economic and social subgroupings, and the civil government within the diverse "worlds of meaning" which have been constituted by the human knower's intentionality in the different cultural epochs through which the human race has passed. To these differences in the nature of the family, the subgroupings, and the state there correspond differences in the nature and the extent of the authority which can be legitimately exercised by each.

Therefore the ethician is no longer free to dispense with the empirical data of history, anthropology, and social science when he is making his moral judgments on contemporary social issues. The epistemological foundations of the fixed social order rooted in the fixed order of nature, on which the old natural law ethicians built their social ethics, have been undermined. But that does not mean that moral reason is now condemned to historicism. Lonergan's distinction between the act of insight and its conceptualization has enabled him to establish that there is an intelligible connection between distinct, successive "worlds of meaning." We should not conclude, however, that the intelligibility of these "worlds of meaning" continually increases with each succeeding epoch. Human history, as we know, consists of cycles of growth and decline; and Lonergan has shown the relation of these cycles to the dialectical opposition between man's pure desire to understand and his other appetites.[31]

The ethician's understanding of this dialectical law, which governs man's intellectual passage from one "world of meaning" to another, can enable him at times to determine whether a given instance of social change indicates an increase or a decline in a society's intelligibility. Thus the admission that our contemporary society belongs to a "new world of meaning" by no means implies that its social structures are exempt from normative evaluation in the light of our historical experience. Nor does it follow that citizens are doing their moral duty when they bow to the demands of their civil governments because these demands are "what the people want today." On the contrary, they may have the duty to criticize the demands of their civil governments on the basis of their own understanding of the dialectical law which governs growth and decline in social intelligibility. Positivist social scientists may dismiss the ethician's effort to make normative judgments about social structures in diverse, evolving "worlds of meaning" as an impossible enterprise. Thomists in the older conceptualist tradition, whose epistemology ignored the intelligible procession of concepts and their frameworks from the act of insight, may have thought that no middle ground existed between social ethics based on fixed natures and pure historicism. Bernard Lonergan's rediscovery of the relation between insight and conceptualization, however, has provided an epistemological foundation on which moral reason's critical evaluation of evolving "worlds of meaning" and their social structures can be built.

In a masterly section of his *Insight*, Lonergan has shown how the critical philosopher, who has understood the dialectical tension between the desire to know and the other appetites in the operation of the incarnate knower, holds the key to a critical philosophy of history and society.[32] This philosopher has become the normative social critic who understands the valid intellectual criteria for judgments of fact and value. He has a firm hold on the norms which should direct intelligent moral conduct. At the same time he has come to understand the human drives which induce men to make unintelligent choices and then to rationalize them as they follow a line of conduct which ultimately leads their society into a long cycle of decline in its intrinsic intelligibility.

RECAPITULATION

The interplay of duty and reason in moral experience reveals that, unless it is impeded, the dynamism of man's intellect and will flowers into a response to God. That free response occurs in an evolving social universe whose "worlds of meaning" succeed each other in history. Since "worlds of meaning" are culturally conditioned, man's duty to respond to God by respecting the intelligible order of values commands his use of moral reason to distinguish the legitimate from the illegitimate demands imposed by their social structures. Transcendental reflection upon the dynamism of man's incarnate spirit is an indispensable prerequisite for making this distinction. The basic unrevisable pattern of social relations grounded in man's spirit condemns the illegitimate usurpation of God's rights and the rights of the family by our contemporary governments. Nonetheless, this unrevisable basic pattern of social relations can assume quite different specifications in diverse "worlds of meaning." Since these specifications are culturally conditioned, their nature and interrelation cannot be understood without empirical inquiry. Man's duty to use moral reason cannot be satisfied if he clings stubbornly to an outmoded ethics whose static pattern of social relations assumes a world of completely fixed natures. Moral reason must admit the fact of historical and cultural evolution. It must strive to understand the *de facto* social structure of our modern world and to observe accurately how cultural and social change have modified the specification of man's basic relations. Moral reason must not be satisfied, however, with a positivistic description of "what actually is." For in the epistemology of the act of insight moral reason has the tool it needs to make normative value judgments about the course of social evolution; and if this be so, the moral axiom "act reasonably" imposes the duty to develop and employ that tool.

But can transcendental Thomism do any more in practice than to ground an admittedly abstract basic pattern of social relations and justify the formal possibility of making normative value judgments about evolving "worlds of meaning"? Have its leading representatives given the ethician any idea of how this type of normative value judgment can be made in practice? Lonergan, it must be admitted, has done comparatively little in this respect. Rahner, on the other hand, has made a number of stimulative suggestions in his more recent articles about the concrete way in which the transcendental Thomist can move from his empirical inquiry into contemporary society to a normative value judgment about a specific issue.

Writing in a theological context, he has shown how transcendental Thomism's epistemology and metaphysics can explain and validate the concrete decisions which groups of Christians or the Church's leaders have the duty to make about specific moral issues at the present moment. More often than not, the complexity of our modern society's culturally conditioned social order precludes the possibility of their reaching clear-cut conclusions through a deductive argument from the general principles of the old natural law social ethics. The relationship between the Church and technical, secularized temporal society is fluctuating and vaguely defined. The ceaseless and rapid evolution of temporal society itself produces a confusing shifting of the relations between families, subsocieties, and governments. It is not easy for moral reason to justify the validity of the urgent practical decisions which must be made about specific issues in the complex, unstable social order. It is even harder for moral reason to determine who has the duty to make these decisions and who has the moral right to require others to follow them.

As a theologian, Rahner may legitimately assume that the Church's leaders, at least in urgent cases, have the duty to make such specific moral decisions and that the Church's members have a corresponding duty to pay heed to them. As a theologian, Rahner can also assume that, since the orders of nature and grace are intrinsically intelligible, Church leaders on whom God has imposed the duty to make concrete moral decisions cannot be lacking in the fundamental ability to arrive at them intelligently. Rahner can then ask the epistemological questions "What type of knowledge is required to make a concrete moral decision about a specific social issue today? How can that type of moral decision be made validly on the basis of our empirical knowledge of our complex, evolving, technical society?"

Rahner replies that the type of knowledge which is needed is a sort of instinct—which, in his theological context, he calls a "faith instinct." [33] This "instinctive knowledge" has affinities to St. Thomas' "knowledge by connaturality." Like prudence, it is a virtue of the practical intellect, acquired or lost through man's habitual moral conduct. Its judgments, which deal with specific cases, are not speculative deductions from general principles. Unlike prudence, however, the "faith instinct" does not restrict its attention to individual, existential moral decisions. The area of its concern is social ethics. The moral instinct is an insight into a specific social situation. The value judgment to which it leads states what is right or wrong "here and now," in this concrete situation. It makes no pronouncement about what is necessarily and eternally right or wrong.

Rahner's later theological writings point out how the Church's increasing use of her "faith instinct" has radically modified the relation of duty and reason in Catholic moral teaching. When the Church is drawing on her faith instinct, as she did in the Pastoral Constitutions of Vatican II, she does not resort to clear-cut condemnations, as she did when she was arguing deductively from fixed first principles. Her teaching takes the form of "prophetic positive recommendations" and the corresponding duty of its hearers is to employ their own moral reason in humble and prayerful consideration of its message.[34] Again, since this moral instinct is "knowledge by connaturality," closely linked to the lived experience of its possessor, we are not surprised that, in the complex, variegated social order of our modern world, the Church's "prophetic positive recommendations" now come more frequently from involved groups of Christians than from the Church's more remote and detached hierarchy.[35]

Rahner has made a notable contribution to Christian ethics by his study of the actual operations of the "faith instinct" in the life of the Catholic Church. He has made a good case for the actual existence of this type of moral instinct. He has also given us some idea of its nature. Nevertheless, a great deal of work remains to be done on the epistemology of this global moral instinct before its possibilities for philosophical ethics can be seriously evaluated. Is it possible to establish the existence of this type of moral instinct by philosophical arguments, in a philosophical context, without drawing on the *a priori* theological presuppositions which Rahner needed to establish it? Does transcendental Thomism have the resources to develop a more satisfactory epistemology of its nature than we find in Rahner's rather sketchy outline? Offhand, it would appear that transcendental Thomism does have these resources. Lonergan's analysis of the human good in *Method of Theology*, his epistemology of the act of insight, and his distinction between "common sense" and "explanatory knowledge" in *Insight* are obvious starting points for an epistemology of the moral instinct. That epistemology has yet to be developed, however, and its contribution to a purely philosophical social ethics remains a promise.

NOTES

1. Jacques Maritain, *The Degrees of Knowledge*, trans. Gerald B. Phelan (New York: Scribner's, 1959).

2. For Karl Rahner's philosophy of God, see *Hearers of the Word*, trans. Michael Richards (New York: Herder & Herder, 1969). A new translation of *Hearers of the Word* by Joseph Donceel, s.j. can be found in *A Rahner Reader*, ed. Gerald A. McCool, s.j. (New York: Seabury, 1975), pp. 2–65. The philosophy of God of the "early Lonergan" can be found in *Insight* (New York: Philosophical Library, 1958), pp. 634–86. For Lonergan's more recent statements on the philosophy of God, see his *Philosophy of God and Theology* (Philadelphia: Westminster, 1973). See also his "Natural Knowledge of God," *A Second Collection*, edd. William F. J. Ryan and Bernard J. Tyrrell (Philadelphia: Westminster, 1974), pp. 117–33.

3. Joseph Maréchal, s.j., *Le Point de départ de la métaphysique*, 3rd ed. (Paris: Desclée de Brouwer, 1944).

4. Joseph de Fever, s.j., *La Preuve réelle de Dieu* (Paris: Desclée de Brouwer, 1953).

5. Henri Bouillard, s.j., *The Knowledge of God* (New York: Herder & Herder, 1968).

6. Joseph Donceel, s.j., *Natural Theology* (New York: Sheed & Ward, 1962).

7. Rahner, *Hearers of the Word*, pp. 34–37. Also in *A Rahner Reader*, pp. 3–6. See also Rahner, *Spirit in the World*, trans. William Dych, s.j. (New York: Herder & Herder, 1957), pp. 57–61.

8. Rahner, "The Theology of Freedom," *Theological Investigations*. VI. *Concerning Vatican Council II* (Baltimore: Helicon, 1969), pp. 178–96, esp. pp. 181–88. Also in *A Rahner Reader*, pp. 255–70.

9. Rahner, *Spirit in the World*, pp. 142–46.

10. Rahner, "Reflections on the Experience of Grace," *Theological Investigations*. III. *The Theology of the Spiritual Life* (Baltimore: Helicon, 1967), pp. 86–90. Also in *A Rahner Reader*, pp. 196–99.

11. Lonergan, *Philosophy of God and Theology*, pp. 53–55.

12. Lonergan, *Method in Theology* (New York: Herder & Herder, 1972).

13. Lonergan, "Dimensions of Meaning," *Collection* (New York: Herder & Herder, 1967).

14. Lonergan, *Insight*, pp. 13–17.

15. Ibid., pp. 191–203, 225–38.

16. Lonergan, "Natural Knowledge of God," pp. 127–34. See also *Method in Theology*, pp. 101–24, 235–66.

17. Rahner, *Hearers of the Word*, pp. 50–52. Also in *A Rahner Reader*, pp. 12–14.

18. Lonergan, *Insight*, pp. 657–58.

19. Rahner, *Hearers of the Word*, pp. 86–89. Also in *A Rahner Reader*, pp. 32–34.

20. In their later works both Lonergan and Rahner, while conceding the autonomy of the philosophical order, locate their own philosophy of God in the context of religious experience.

21. For Rahner's defense of a basic natural law ethics, see "On the Question of a Formal Existential Ethics," *Theological Investigations*. II. *Man in the Church* (Baltimore: Helicon, 1963), pp. 217–34, esp. 218–22, 224–29, 231–34. Also in *A Rahner Reader*, pp. 245–54.

22. Rahner, *Hearers of the Word*, pp. 121–29. Also in *A Rahner Reader*, pp. 48–55.

23. Lonergan, *Doctrinal Pluralism* (Milwaukee: Marquette University Press, 1971), p. 8. See also *Method in Theology*, p. 20.

24. Rahner, "The Dignity and Freedom of Man," *Theological Investigations* II, pp. 235–63, esp. pp. 236–41, 248–52. Also in *A Rahner Reader*, pp. 262–270.

25. Rahner, "Ideology and Christianity," *Theological Investigations* VI, pp. 43–58, esp. pp. 43–45, 52–57. Also in *A Rahner Reader*, pp. 337–42.

26. Lonergan, *Insight*, pp. 619–24.

27. Rahner, "Dignity and Freedom of Man," pp. 249–52.

28. Rahner, "The Experiment with Man," *Theological Investigations*. IX. *Writings of 1965–67* I (London: Darton, Longman & Todd, 1972), pp. 205–24.

29. Lonergan, *Doctrinal Pluralism*, pp. 8–12.

30. Lonergan, "Dimensions of Meaning," pp. 252–67.

31. Lonergan, *Insight*, pp. 225–38.

32. Ibid.

33. Rahner, "The Problem of Genetic Manipulation," *Theological Investigations* IX, pp. 225–52, esp. pp. 227–28, 230–31. Also in *A Rahner Reader*, pp. 270–77.

34. Rahner, "On the Theological Problems Entailed in a 'Pastoral Constitution,' " *Theological Investigations. X. Writings of 1965–67* II (London: Darton, Longman & Todd, 1973), pp. 293–317.

35. Rahner, "The Function of the Church as a Critic of Society," *Theological Investigations. XIII. Theology, Anthropology, Christology* (London: Darton, Longman & Todd, 1975), pp. 229–49.

9

Freedom from the Good

CHARLES A. KELBLEY

MY PURPOSE IN THIS PAPER is to explore the basis of a thesis which I believe underlies much of John Rawls's *A Theory of Justice*,[1] the proposition that in a well-organized and just society a genuine freedom for the good presupposes a prior freedom from the good. I hope to show that understanding the basis for such a proposition can be quite important for our society, not only because it might help us to appreciate a major work of contemporary moral philosophy, but also because it might give us some insight into the kinds of considerations which are relevant to reconciling different sorts of opposing claims and conflicts concerning freedom, justice, equality, and the good life. As we move through our bicentennial year we are being given many opportunities to reflect upon what our freedom is for and the many things we are free from. But we seldom stop to reflect upon the deeper basis of our various freedoms, assuming for the moment that we truly have them. Worse, we may be so self-satisfied with our freedoms and what they are for that we unwittingly acquiesce in ways of life which are more restricting and perhaps more damaging to our moral nature than we would either suspect prior to reflection or accept if we were to reflect long and hard enough on the nature of freedom, goodness, and justice.

John Rawls's long reflections on the nature of justice have resulted in a profound and complex theory, which he often characterizes as a conception of justice founded upon a certain priority of the right over the good. This is the broader context in which I shall locate my own discussion of freedom. Although Rawls's position concerning the priority of the right over the good does not exactly correspond to what I shall mean by "freedom from the good," it nonetheless contains the basic grounds for viewing freedom in this particular way. As I see it, I shall simply be giving expression to what is already implicit, if not explicit, in Rawls's discussion of the priority of the right, although, needless to say, there may be points on which I go further than Rawls would care to go—or, indeed, points on which I place insufficient emphasis.[2]

In order to prepare the way for this exploration I shall outline the nature of the problem as I see it in the first part of the essay and then discuss a few of the relevant concepts of Rawls's theory in the second part. The reader who is already familiar with this powerful theory will doubtless agree that making a sketch of it is a risky enterprise which is bound to pose more questions than it answers. In presenting this sketch, I therefore ask the reader to bear in mind that I wish to establish a general background for a fairly limited purpose and do not propose to assess the overall argument of *A Theory of Justice*. Yet, against this background, the bearings of the various relations between the concepts of the right and the good on the correctness of Rawls's theory in general can, I think, be better appreciated (as I try to show more systematically in the last two parts).

I want to stress that I shall not be attempting to probe in depth any of the more particular doctrines of *A Theory of Justice*, which would presuppose that the reader already have a fairly good grasp of it.[3] My aim is both more modest and more ambitious: to present and explore a thesis which animates the work as a whole. I might add that I shall have relatively little to say about the nature of either freedom or the good, which may seem surprising in view of the article's title. Were it not for the possibility that such a discussion would involve patent nonsense, I should risk saying that the article is mostly about the "from" in the title. Instead I shall, more sensibly, say that the central thing is the relation *between* freedom and the good.

I

One of the exceptional traits of *A Theory of Justice* is its attempt to reverse or to alter substantially the relationship between the concepts of the right and the good as these function in the formulas of moral philosophy. According to Rawls, the main lines of traditional moral philosophy have been dominated by concepts of the good defined prior to and independently of a concept of the right. It is Rawls's dissatisfaction with the moral consequences of this relationship which leads him to seek an alternative to a leading exponent of the priority of the good, utilitarianism. Now, utilitarianism has commonly defined the right as the maximization of a previously defined good. One can see this priority of the good clearly embedded in the succinct statement of the principle of utility which Francis Hutcheson formulated in 1725: "That action is best, which procures the greatest happiness for the greatest numbers; and that, worst, which, in like manner, occasions misery." [4] To the extent that a utilitarian such as John Stuart Mill held the similar view that utility or "the greatest happiness principle" is the foundation of morals, the test or criterion of right or wrong, to that extent the good had clear priority over the right.

An extremely abbreviated account of the procedure of utilitarianism might thus consist in noting that it begins by defining the good for society, determining the aims which should be pursued for its members; and then proceeds to define the right as the maximization of this concept of the good. But this is actually a somewhat misleading characterization of utilitarianism since it says nothing of the way in which the good was arrived at in order to be defined. Neither Mill nor Bentham, for example, defines the good on arbitrary grounds. Mill will claim that the principle of utility governs what men do in fact seek in their actions, so that utility is merely *descriptive* of human behavior. Of course, where the utilitarians may appear to be on shaky ground is in claiming that the factual desires of people are evidential grounds for what they *ought* to desire. But rather than go into this issue here I shall simply admit that full justice cannot be done to the complexities of utilitarianism within the framework of this article.

At any rate, in accordance with the principle of utility, rightness consists in whatever produces the greatest good for the greatest number. Now, it might be thought that in this formulation the right and the good are actually defined simultaneously. But I believe that the right (the greatest) must be seen as merely adjectival to the good and dependent upon it. Moreover, the concept of greatest (or the idea of maximization) is clearly not a necessary component of the concept of the right, which suggests that the right can be independent of the good, although it happens not to be so in the utilitarian tradition. To be sure, the utilitarian's way of linking the right and the good may seem natural enough if ethics begins with the good and *then* seeks a definition of the right. Given such a starting point, the basis for thinking that this association is natural lies simply in the fact that we then tend to think of the good as something which should be maximized, more of a good being better than less.[5]

It would surely be a mistake to allow what has been said to obscure the fact that utilitarianism, too, seeks justice. It must be remembered that utilitarianism is actually an alternate theory of justice, summarized in the principle of utility. Thus when the utilitarian defines the right as the maximization of the good, he may be thought of as saying that this is the best way to promote justice. He has the good of society, of the greatest number, at heart. Again, I do not want to nor can I engage in either an attack on or a defense of utilitarianism here. But on the positive side it could be argued that utilitarianism holds up to us a lofty conception of morality since it demands more of a self-sacrifice for some individuals (the minority not included in the greatest number) than is required by Rawls's theory of justice. Whether such a sacrifice is right or just is, of course, another question; in fact it is a main one for Rawls.[6]

Now, admittedly, there is a strong intuitive appeal in a procedure which makes the right or obligation dependent upon a prior determination of the good. It is the appeal of a teleological theory of moral obligation, which holds, as one author puts it, that "the basic or ultimate criterion or standard of what is morally right, wrong, obligatory, etc., is the nonmoral value that is brought into being."[7] Teleological theories thus make the right or the obligatory dependent on the good—the nonmoral good, by which is meant such things as pleasure, power, knowledge, perfection, self-realization, etc., things which it may be morally good to *pursue* but which, in and of themselves, are neither moral nor immoral, morality having to do with persons, actions, motives, etc.[8] The appeal of a teleological theory of moral obligation also lies in the common sense conviction that it is nearly impossible to engage in any discussion of the right— for example, a right action—unless one first knows *what* it is good to do. In other words, the right may seem impossibly abstract without a prior knowledge of the good. As we shall see, Rawls will partially, but only partially, concede this point.[9]

Given the *prima facie* appeal of the priority of good, it should be noted that as a consequence of this priority one not only is deprived of an independent concept of the right; one may also be denied the freedom to implement a conception of the good if it is incompatible with the dominant conception of the good in a particular society. To appreciate the political significance of this point, it suffices to recall that many social systems, past and present, have been literally obsessed with the imposition of a narrowly defined conception of social good on its citizens. In this respect it would seem quite possible for a totalitarian regime to use to its own advantage the seemingly neutral descriptions of human desires and even the overtones of majoritarian democracy found in utilitarianism, for it often seems that utilitarians believe that everyone does in fact have or ought to have the same desires and goals. But this is not to say that excellent reasons could not be given to support even a severely restricted conception of social good at a particular level of civilization. Yet the philosophical significance of this point is much greater and lies in the fact that, in addition to justifying the obvious oppressions of some social systems, a dominant conception of social good can silently infiltrate the economic and political institutions of an otherwise democratic society and provide the background conditions which set the stage for the terms in which most people will conceive their life plans and what they can hope to accomplish. If the good sets the stage for the definition of the right, then what is the right will implicitly define some putative goods as wrong, possibly on quite arbitrary grounds. It is only too obvious that all this can have deep and pervasive effects on the identity and socialization processes without so much as a murmur of suspicion or revolt from a society's members. This is the problematic impact of the priority-of-the-good position and why, as a consequence, we must ask whether we can accept it on moral grounds. Should the right be determined by the good and be its servant, performing the function of maximization? Should not the right be independent of the good? For if it is not, then the right becomes, so to speak, powerless to make a principled evaluation of the good. The question is whether we can live with the consequences of such a weak concept of the right.

Based on considerations such as the above, *A Theory of Justice* attempts to define an alternative to the utilitarian conception of justice and begins by trying to establish an independent basis for principles of the right prior to the consideration of any major concept of the good. I say "major" because in fact Rawls uses a minimal conception of the good which actually does precede and influence in some sense his theory of justice. That is, he has to rely upon what he calls "primary goods" and a "thin theory of the good" in order to be able to formulate any principles of justice at all. This is the sense in which Rawls might be said to concede that the right is impossibly abstract without a prior knowledge of the good. Yet he argues that this procedure, to which I shall return later, does not really compromise an independent conception of the right. It seems clear, then, that in Rawls's view genuine social freedom will be dependent upon a prior freedom from the good, or at least upon a freedom from a "full" or dominant conception of the good. A person can be free for something only by first being free from something.[10]

There are also fairly solid intuitive grounds for the primacy and priority of the right over the good. In conjunction with what has already been said, this appeal consists primarily in the principle that the good, whatever it is, must be able to be judged by criteria other than factual human desires, even if these desires are shared by the vast majority. But even if we concede that the desires of the "greatest number" of individuals may be for what is *good*, still, it is not necessarily *right* to allow majority desires to prevail. For as Rawls will maintain, ultimately something is morally good if, and only if, it is consistent with the principles of the right.

In terms of conventional ethical theories, the appeal here is that of a deontological theory of moral obligation, which "contends that it is possible for an action or rule of action to be the morally right or obligatory one even if it does not promote the greatest balance of good over evil for self, society, or universe. It may be right or obligatory simply because of some other fact about it or because of its own nature." [11] A deontological theory, therefore, stresses considerations other than the goals, values, or consequences of an act, considerations such as the nature or the rationality of the act itself. Kant's categorical imperative is certainly one of the classical expressions of a deontological theory of moral obligation, for he insisted that the desire for the good and for happiness in general must be completely divorced from the concepts of duty and the right—which does not mean, of course, that happiness and consequences are irrelevant to a moral point of view. In this connection—the details of Rawls's complicated relations with Kant and the nature and extent of the latter's deontology aside—it is necessary to avoid the impression (which is not an uncommon one of Kant) that Rawls minimizes the importance of the good. The right and the good being the two most fundamental concepts of ethics, it is a question of establishing their relationship, and for Rawls this relationship is primarily defined in terms of the priority of the right. Still, given this priority, it is noteworthy that approximately one-third of *A Theory of Justice* is devoted to developing a theory of the good and to determining the way in which this theory is congruent with the right and justice. If a theory of the right and principles of justice are not congruent with human good, that for Rawls is a sufficient reason to reject them. In presenting his theory of justice as a deontological theory, Rawls is therefore careful to note that such theories are not "views that characterize the rightness of institutions and acts independently from their consequences. All ethical doctrines worth our attention take consequences into account in judging rightness. One which did not would simply be irrational, crazy." [12] Thus an ethics must always be concerned with both the right and the good. To ignore one or the other is to misrepresent and disfigure the comprehensive nature of ethical concern as well as the nature of moral personality (moral persons for Rawls being defined as rational individuals with a capacity for a sense of justice *and* a conception of their good or of a coherent system of ends).

It can be seen that the above discussion merely suggests the dimensions of the problem of establishing the priority of either the right or the good. Since some limits have to be drawn for this paper, I am not able to make even a complete sketch of the problem. But on the basis of this brief background I shall now present the more specific context of *A Theory of Justice* which demands the priority of the right or, as I prefer to think of it, an initial freedom from the good.

II

A Theory of Justice is an extraordinarily difficult work to characterize in any summary fashion and still remain faithful to its complexity—not only because it has so many themes and facets, all united to the concept of justice, so many tangents which cross the boundaries of other disciplines (assimilating portions of economics and psychology, for example, to the quest for justice), but also because it is written with a great deal of respect for the enormous task of defining a concept of justice without ignoring, or, even worse, denying, the inputs which must come from other areas of philosophy and from other disciplines. Consequently, Rawls writes in a style which is somewhat tentative; conclusions, even major ones, are frequently softened by *caveat*s regarding the missing details or the further analysis which would be needed in a complete version of an account of justice. Bearing this in mind, I should like to characterize Rawls's work very freely and, of course, very partially in terms of three headings: "justice as fairness," the "original position," and the "social contract." The discussion of each of these headings will sometimes overlap the others and point to other concepts and topics. Yet I believe that, taken as a whole, they contribute the major support for the idea that principles of justice require freedom from the good.

The overall label for Rawls's theory is justice as fairness, from which one might be led to conclude that justice will be defined as fairness. At times it may seem that Rawls's search for justice is actually a search for a suitable definition of fairness, that he is trying to substitute fairness for justice. But since the concept of justice is often thought of as virtually synonymous with the concept of fairness, this would not seem to constitute a constructive procedure. Why the label "justice as fairness"? Is justice not fairness itself? I think that the radical nature of Rawls's concept of fairness cannot be understood and distinguished from the concept of justice unless it is first seen in the light of the "original position," to which I now turn in order to elucidate the concept of fairness.

The original position is Rawls's particular interpretation of a hypothetical initial situation which roughly corresponds to what earlier social contract doctrines called "the state of nature." In general, the original position is intended to represent the moral standpoint according to which individuals are assumed to be behind a "veil of ignorance" concealing from them certain information about themselves, their identity and the nature of their conceptions of the good. In this non-historical and purely hypothetical situation, individuals are to choose principles of justice under identical circumstances, and their major circumstance is a lack of self-knowledge. To be sure, in order to choose a viable conception of justice they must know certain things about society and human psychology. But these are general things and do not tell them who they are or what they are like. What they lack is information of the kind which one could summarize under the heading of individual psychology and which ordinarily exerts some influence on the choice of principles of justice.

It is most important that individuals entering the original position should be viewed as ignorant of their own conceptions of the good. For if in any group of individuals there are always several conceptions of the good, then this is surely a circumstance which would promote disagreement on the principles of justice. The original position is a simplifying device which is required to define fair principles of justice on the prior basis of a fair set of conditions. The idea is that a fair result can be the outcome only of a fair procedure which sets the stage for judgment, just as a substantive decision on justice in a criminal trial, say, is founded on a fair set of procedures with respect to evidence, testimony, inference, etc., such procedures constituting an indispensable basis for a fair verdict. One of the fair conditions required by the original position is, therefore, the elimination in thought of an individual's conception of the good. Rawls wants to show that it is not our aims, or our conceptions of the good, which exclusively reveal our moral nature; that is only half the story. According to the priority-of-the-right doctrine, our moral nature is revealed first and foremost by "the principles that we would acknowledge to govern the background conditions under which these aims are to be pursued." [13]

There is a clear sense, then, in which the good can confuse and distort the meaning of justice: it is the sense in which contingent or accidental qualities become confused with the essence of a thing, or in which facts get translated into norms and principles. In the Husserlian language of phenomenological reduction: the parties in the original position are forced to "bracket" the factual aspects of their personal lives in order to focus on the "essence" of fairness in the human condition. If the facts characterizing one individual's life are used as a basis for judgment on principles of justice, this may be (to borrow again from Husserlian language) nothing more than a "prejudice of the world," a manifestation of the "natural attitude." Similarly, Rawls's conception of fairness requires a correction of the "arbitrariness of the world," by which he means the chance ways in which society and natural endowment have favored some individuals with more advantageous starting points. Here again the original position is comparable to Husserlian reduction in that it is a striking movement away from natural and social facts. Justice will not be found in the natural and social worlds.

There are other aspects of the rationale which require the deliberators in the original position to suspend their conceptions of the good. Here I shall focus on just one more, but one which I think is quite instructive for evaluating the "freedom from the good" position. Rawls supposes that rational and mutually disinterested persons (not to be confused with egoists) realize that they must not jeopardize their eventual dispositional or hypothetical freedoms by using a particular conception of the good in the original position.[14] For if they do not know what their conception of the good will actually be once the veil of ignorance is lifted, they cannot risk accepting any conceptions of the good as a premiss in deciding principles of justice. Although Rawls tends to view a theory of justice as part of the theory of rational choice, such that justice will be *decided* by what it would be *rational* to choose under the conditions of the original position, it does not seem to be the case that fairness (or the conditions of the original position) can be entirely or even primarily a result of strict rationality, since one does not reason to these conditions. In effect, Rawls wants to show that fairness demands that we confront ourselves, so to speak, as we really are, that is, independent of the donations of nature and nurture. Yet this is not an appeal to rationality but a reference to values which are brought into the theory, as it were, from the outside. The difficulty is removed when one realizes that there are two separate arguments, both of which relate to freedom from the good: one concerning fairness and another concerning justice; this allows us to split Rawls's theory into two parts, one concerned with the core of the original position (fairness) and the other with the choices and decisions made in the original position (justice). The argument concerned with justice may be primarily a matter of determining what it is strictly rational to choose given the circumstances of the original position. But the argument concerning fairness is not dependent upon the nature of rationality. That is, in order to define fairness, Rawls relies on moral convictions which are independent of his theory, convictions which he believes are generally fixed and firm for all, or nearly all, men. Thus the novelty of justice as fairness is the systematic way in which Rawls defines fairness, employing what he believes are humanity's firm moral convictions about fairness, and then rigorously deriving the principles of justice from the conditions which define fairness. In sum, fairness requires freedom from the good, i.e., requires me to put out of play the contingencies of my own life, contingencies which normally set the stage for my aims and for what I consider good: and then, given my condition of fairness, *rationality* will dictate that the other deliberators on justice and I refrain from using any concept of the good in determining the principles of justice. It is important to keep these two arguments separate, for, as Rawls recognizes, it is possible to accept his position on fairness while rejecting his position on justice, and vice versa. It may be worth noting that if one does reject his principles of justice, one may still have to accept his fairness doctrine and then decide what notion of justice would derive from it. But, in any event, the point I wish to make is that the "freedom from the good" position can be attached to both of Rawls's arguments, to the idea of fairness and to the concept of rationality which is used to choose the principles of justice.

It would not be accurate to say, as I may have seemed to suggest just now, that both fairness and justice require freedom from the good. Strictly speaking, fairness and rationality require it, but the latter requires it only because fairness does. Thus, because rationality operates on the foundation of fairness, and assimilates, as it were, the condition of freedom from the good, it can translate this condition into the resulting principles of justice. Justice does not require freedom from the good; it embodies it, at least if we are speaking of justice *as fairness*.

From this it can be seen that freedom from the good depends more crucially on the fairness doctrine of the original position than it does on Rawls's view of rationality. For if it were not for the fairness of the original position, rationality would be faced with other data and premises from which to reason on justice.

In view of this, I shall return to an aspect of what Rawls believes is demanded by fairness.

It does not require much reading between the lines to say that *A Theory of Justice* suggests [15] that many existing societies have failed to deal justly with natural and social contingencies. Simply to take such contingencies as a point of departure for deciding issues of justice, of what is *due* a person, is to make a virtue out of arbitrariness. For if there is no way in which a person can be said to merit or deserve such assets or defects, if they are the outcome of the natural and social lotteries, as Rawls believes, then any use of them is unfair and consequently unjust: unfair, since persons in an original position of equality would not agree that someone could deserve the advantages or disadvantages which customarily go with native or social endowments; unjust, because the results which flow from using them were determined on an unfair basis. It should be noted that Rawls is not arguing that inequalities are unjust; he is trying to show that their influence should be mitigated. As he points out, what nature has conferred upon us is neither just nor unjust; it is the way in which we deal with these facts which is just or unjust.[16] Thus Rawls seeks to define the conditions under which one can enjoy inequalities according to a reasonable standard. What is a reasonable standard? One which would be chosen from a position which does not allow the use of self-knowledge.

Now, it is easy to see that although Rawls is speaking of what the deliberators in the original position would find it reasonable to think about merit and desert, this argument is also meant to appeal to *our* sense of fairness and our considered judgments on arbitrariness. Using distance from arbitrariness as a measure for a superior theory of justice, Rawls can claim that his own is superior to theories such as natural liberty, natural aristocracy, and liberal equality; for in these theories the natural is a "given" which seems to need little justification or regulation.[17] (The extent to which these theories do regulate natural or social contingencies is the basis for their distinction from each other.) But, again, rather than basing justice on facts, Rawls wants to claim that the principles of justice are to be regarded as an object of an agreement which is to be made prior to knowledge of the facts concerning an individual's natural and social characteristics. Rawls, after all, is propounding a contract theory of justice, and agreement is an indispensable part of any contract theory.

The sense in which Rawls's theory follows or departs from the social contract tradition may constitute one of the most interesting aspects of his thought. It is clear that there are sharp differences beween Rawls and Locke, Rousseau, and Kant, but I am not able to discuss his relationship to this tradition here. Suffice it to say that his theory is contractarian because of the image, fostered by the original position, of men agreeing to a contract outside of, although not prior to, an organized social schema, a contract which sets down the most general principles of their relations, specifying such things as rights and duties, liberties and powers, the conditions under which one may enjoy certain advantages in income and wealth, etc. Again, the idea is that men are to agree upon the principles of their association in society, not that they could ever in fact do so, for here we are not discussing facts but an ideal which rational individuals can embrace as a standard against which to measure the moral nature of social institutions and efforts at reform.

The rationale for this agreement or contract reveals again the Kantian nature of Rawls's theory: only in this way are persons acting autonomously, giving laws to themselves, expressing their nature as free and equal rational beings. Behind the contract view lies the powerful idea that persons are to base their social morality on principles which they derive from their own nature. But before these persons can decide upon these principles of social morality, their natures must be purified, so to speak, of all contingent facts so that the eventual agreement will give expression to their common nature and not to the arbitrariness of the world. The contract idea sets this theory in motion: the social bond is not to be secured by coercion or justified by arbitrary facts but by means of a free and rational consent which reflects one's equality with all others. But in order to define a fair contract one must first define a fair basis for making a contract, and this is where the original position becomes so important.

Once the original position is suitably defined to represent fair conditions for judgment, conditions under which no one would have a basis in knowledge for choosing principles of justice favorable to oneself, then the choice for principles would lead almost by deductive necessity to Rawls's own two principles: the principle of equal liberty and the "difference principle," according to which social and economic inequalities are justified if they are to everyone's advantage. I shall not discuss the complexities of his two principles here since my purpose is not to assess the particular doctrines of his theory but a key position on the good which provides much of the support for that theory.[18]

Before concluding this partial sketch of Rawls's theory, I shall present one additional perspective from which to view "freedom from the good." The idea of pure procedural justice plays an important role in Rawls's work from the very outset. It can be best understood by first contrasting it with perfect and imperfect procedural justice.[19] Perfect procedural justice can be illustrated in an elementary way by the problem of equitably dividing a cake. We know what end we want (an equal division) independent of any procedure to get there; and we know of a procedure which is sure to reach this end: for example, asking one man to cut the cake and to take the last piece, which procedure assumes that he wants at least an equal share of the cake and that he can and will divide the cake equally so that the last piece, whichever it is, is at least as large as the others. Thus the essence of perfect procedural justice consists in having an independent criterion of a just outcome and being able to secure a procedure which is sure to reach that end. By contrast, imperfect procedural justice is exemplified by a criminal trial, and although it also has an independent criterion of a just outcome (that criminals, say, should be found guilty) there are only imperfect means (a fallible jury system) to attain this end. Since it cannot guarantee the independently defined goal, it is therefore *imperfect* procedural justice. It is clear that perfect procedural justice is rare and that imperfect procedural justice is characteristic of the criminal and civil justice systems which attempt to cope with violations of laws. But if we assume that laws are based on justice, then the ends which laws are looking to attain have their *raison d'être* in a substantive concept of justice which antedates the laws. Now, Rawls wants to claim that justice, in its original form, is a matter of pure procedural justice which, as the phrase suggests, is purely procedural since it has no independent criterion for a right or just result: "instead there is a correct or fair procedure such that the outcome is likewise correct or fair, whatever it is, provided that the procedure has been properly followed."[20] Rawls illustrates pure procedural justice with gambling, but the notion is found in his theory as early as the original position, where, as I am emphasizing, there is no independent criterion of what constitutes justice. Indeed, this is the whole point behind the original position, the veil of ignorance, and the social contract. In the original position, understood as the strictly moral posture, we reflect on justice with no prior ends in view:

> the aim is to characterize this situation so that the principles that would be chosen, whatever they turn out to be, are acceptable from a moral point of view. The original position is defined in such a way that it is a status quo in which any agreements reached are fair. It is a state of affairs in which the parties are equally represented as moral persons and the outcome is not conditioned by arbitrary contingencies or the relative balance of social forces. Thus justice as fairness is able to use the idea of pure procedural justice from the beginning.[21]

Perhaps as well as anything in *A Theory of Justice*, this text expresses Rawls's deontology and, at the same time, the priority-of-the-right and the "freedom from the good" positions.

III

From out of the above sketch I should like to isolate three theses which, although not necessarily defended in each case by Rawls explicitly, do seem to bear heavily on the validity of "freedom from the good" or priority-of-the-right claims: (1) conceptions of human good are not contingently but necessarily multiple and heterogeneous; (2) conceptions of the good cannot be ranked in a hierarchy and used in political principles without violating justice, the hypothetical liberties of all citizens, and the nature of the person as a rational being; (3) the priority of the good is irrational, and this can be seen best from the original position perspective. I shall make several comments in this section on the first two theses and discuss the third in the final section.

The first thesis asserts not merely that conceptions of human good are contingently heterogeneous, the result, for example, of incomplete information, erroneous judgment, lack of education, and so forth; but, rather, that the good is necessarily diverse and should not be conceived as containing a single homogeneous content. Rawls's assertion that "human good is heterogeneous because the aims of the self are heterogeneous" [22] certainly shows that he is in accord with this thesis. But perhaps the heterogeneity of human good takes on significance especially in terms of Rawls's conception of society as a social union.[23] Now, this conception holds that each member of society, taken as an individual, is doomed to incompletion and partial cultivation. Self-realization, in the sense of becoming complete and whole, everything that one can be, is an illusory ideal, rampant though it may be in some current psychologies. In Rawls's idea of social union, each person is seen as but a fragment of what he or she might be or could potentially be. Normal human life spans or even several lifetimes are never sufficient to develop all of one individual's powers and capacities. Each person is, in an important sense, a society "writ small," [24] teeming with possible selves and potential developments which, for the individual alone, must tragically be left unrealized. Fortunately, through union with other people one achieves a certain realization of those portions of the self which otherwise would never be experienced and thereby participates in the full and potentially complete expression of human nature.

The fact that no one person can ever exhaust the possible degrees of self-development in the numberless ways of living and seeking good suggests that each one of us has an essential limit which is not erased by either social union or indefinite time. Even if each single person should contain the fullest possible range of powers and capacities (an extremely implausible assumption), it would still appear impossible for him to realize them all completely, exhausting all the possibilities of rational life without remainder. It follows that one person cannot experience the human essence through union with others either, thus canceling the idea that we are only contingently incomplete until we pass through social union. On the contrary, the idea of social union would seem to demand that we conceive of our interdependence as an essential and necessary one, something we can never grow out of except at the price of severing ourselves from the human milieu.

A diversity of conceptions of the good is, therefore, far from being a defect for society. Indeed, the attempt to destroy this diversity surely reflects the totalitarian impulse to assimilate otherness into sameness, an impulse which is linked with the philosophical or political decision to allow, or acquiesce unwittingly in, the priority of the good. Rawls's conception of society as a social union, therefore, requires a diversity of conceptions of the good on the ground that only in this way can the self find a context in which to achieve a certain kind of wholeness through union with others.[25]

The second thesis denies that there is a method for ranking conceptions of the good in terms of a hierarchy. This follows in part from the first thesis, which throws doubt upon any principle of perfection which is used as a political principle [26] on the ground that plurality, diversity, and perhaps even conflict, are necessary to the fullest expression of human nature. It may be worth recalling that, inasmuch as principles of the right or justice are already on hand, there is a way to deal with conflicts which arise from a diversity of conceptions of the good.

But, more importantly, any such hierarchy would seem to violate the first of Rawls's two principles of justice, the equal liberty principle. For liberty, I take it, should be conceived as a state in which, supported by background institutions, a person has the greatest possible number of potential or hypothetical powers, opportunities, and rights which are reasonably consistent with a like liberty for all others; but the requirement to seek one end or to follow one conception of the good is antithetical to this concept of liberty. I emphasize the hypothetical or dispositional nature of liberty inasmuch as this sense includes all possible but not necessarily actual or even probable human desires; and I do so because, as is often said, merely possible desires have a way of becoming actual.[27] Now, a commitment to a certain conception of the good prior to a conception of the right would seem to violate the provision for equal hypothetical liberties, and there is no justification for this short of the totalitarian impulse to assimilate otherness into sameness.[28]

These considerations move us naturally toward the last part of the second thesis, according to which the priority of the good violates the nature of man as a rational being. Here it is a question not merely of violating the principle of equal liberty, but of violating the very nature of the person. A moral person, for Rawls, has the capacity for a conception of the good and the capacity for a sense of justice. Given the constraints imposed by the priority of the right, any conception of the good is equal to any other life plan which is also consistent with principles of the right. Further, in light of the idea of social union and its roots in human nature, a rational being must depend upon an indefinite number of life plans complementary to his own. If a single conception of the good should become the necessary end of a society, then this is obviously at odds with the nature of rationality and human nature.

We see in Kant an awareness of the same difficulty of the priority-of-the-good position. Kant says that "Men have different views on the empirical end of happiness and what it consists of, so that as far as happiness is concerned, their will cannot be brought under any common principle nor thus under any external law harmonizing the freedom of everyone." [29] I take it that Kant also means that a common principle of justice will be impossible to settle upon so long as it is sought among the empirical choices and definitions of the good which people in fact have. Here one can find no necessity or compelling *commonality*, one capable of "harmonizing the freedom of everyone." For happiness and the good, like all human ends, can be part of a moral point of view only on the prior basis of a conception of the right.

IV

I shall now discuss the third thesis, which states that the priority of the good is irrational and that this can be seen best from the perspective of the original position. We may note first that for Rawls a consideration of principles of the right cannot really get under way unless some conception of the good is known by the deliberators in the original position. The reason for this is that the deliberators, lacking all information about the content of human desires, would have insufficient grounds for choosing between competing theories of justice. We must remember that a critical idea of the original position is precisely not to let individuals know their substantive convictions about the good, the aims and purposes which they have in real life. Still, unless they have some conception of what people in general desire, their principles of justice may turn out to be inapplicable to human beings. To meet this problem, Rawls introduces a minimal conception of the good into the original position. But the question arises: What notion of the good can be used which would not be controversial and which would not jeopardize the possibility of a unanimous choice on justice? Rawls argues that the principles of justice should apply to "primary goods," which include liberties and rights, powers and opportunities, income and wealth, and, most important of all, self-respect. The assumption is that it is rational to want these primary goods as means of pursuing any substantive ends, no matter what they turn out to be once the veil of ignorance is lifted. This minimal concept of the good acts as a kind of guide to the concept of the right; but it does so, Rawls believes, without compromising the independence of the right.

In defense of this claim one could argue that primary goods do not implicate a relationship to specific ends or goals; they are simply the normally indispensable means to achieve any substantive end whatever. Even if one should want to become a hermit and to lead a contemplative life on the top of an isolated mountain, it is necessary to have the liberty, power, and whatever means are necessary to do this, as well as the liberty to renounce productive work, possessions, and worldly pleasure. At the same time, a rational hermit might wish to secure in advance the hypothetical future liberty to renounce his unusual way of life and to re-enter more normal ways of living.

Thus the deliberators, deprived of their own conception of the good and their own particular life plans, would find it rational to choose their principles of justice at least in view of this minimal conception of the good, the reason being, once again, that they need to have some conception of what they want as human beings.[30] But I contend that they would find it irrational to define principles of justice on the basis of any more substantive conception of the good. Now, I believe that this is not necessarily Rawls's explicit point of view. If I am correct, he would say, not that it would be *irrational* for the parties in the original position to employ a more substantive idea of the good, but rather that, in virtue of the constraints on knowledge, it is merely impossible to do so.

These are two rather different claims, and though Rawls's claim is a consequence of the conditions of the original position, it is likely to be seen as a result of a merely artificial logic. Although Rawls emphasizes the hypothetical nature of the original position, there can be no doubt that it is intended to represent in some sense a moral point of view. But this is problematic on at least two counts. First, it seems preferable to argue that, from the moral point of view, it is irrational to choose principles of justice on the basis of any substantive view of the good, rather than to argue that it is merely impossible to do so. For in a moral posture, where freedom exists, it is necessary to have options. Rawls would therefore be making a rather weak claim if he means that the moral point of view, represented by the original position, makes it impossible to employ a substantive conception of the good. Secondly, there is an ambiguity about how we are to understand the moral point of view in relation to the original position. In one sense, it *is* irrational for the deliberators to decide justice on the basis of a substantive idea of the good, precisely because in so doing they might be compromising their own best interests which, in the original position, they are ignorant of. Under conditions of uncertainty, one makes decisions so as to maximize the minimal outcome. Now, while this is the notion of rationality which Rawls is using in the original position, it is not a concept of rationality which one would normally associate with a moral point of view. Where, one might wonder, is the morality of the deliberators in the original position? Surely it is not found in sufficient depth in their concept of rationality, for that seems to be a purely instrumental notion of rationality.[31]

Here it is helpful to recall that Rawls has two separate arguments at work regarding the original position, one on fairness, the other on justice. The argument on fairness constructs a moral point of view out of moral convictions which seem to be independent of the theory of justice. Now, given the moral foundations of fairness, which require, among other things, freedom from the good, it would be irrational to decide principles of justice on the basis of any substantive idea of the good. But this is not the line of reasoning which Rawls adopts for the deliberators in the original position. For they are concerned not with fairness but only with justice and with how they can think their way out of the position they are in with the least amount of damage. Although the deliberators are rational, at least in one sense of the term, they do not appear to have an opinion about the moral nature of the fairness condition, and this makes it difficult for us to view *them* as truly occupying a moral standpoint.

Despite these difficulties, I believe that my contention can still be seen as basically compatible with an original position doctrine on the moral reasoning of the deliberators. Thus, while these deliberators are perforce ignorant of their own substantive ideas of the good, one of the pieces of information which are available to them is that the world contains a plurality of conceptions of the good, as well as many philosophical and political doctrines. Now, given the constraints on self-knowledge, they would know that any choice for principles which favor a particular view of the good, be it pleasure, power, wealth, or spirituality, could very easily go against their own best interests in everyday life. This is the line of reasoning which Rawls develops. But I believe that they must also realize that a choice for one conception of the good would compromise conceptions embraced by other people. Granted: Rawls does not allow altruism to play a role in the original position—and with reason. He emphasizes instead the motive of mutual disinterest, which amounts to an unselfish self-interest. But it would seem impossible for the deliberators to act either for or against their own self-interest since, according to the hypothesis of the original position, they do not know their own selves, and what they do not know they surely cannot knowingly act against. True, each deliberator knows he is somebody, but to act in the name of somebody in general and no one in particular does not seem to fall under behavior which can meaningfully be called self-interested. Therefore I believe one is led to the conclusion that in virtue of the very conditions of the original position a choice for principles of right based on a substantive concept of the good would in fact be against the interests of all people and therefore perceived as irrational. In sum, to adopt the priority-of-the-good position amounts to compromising the nature of rationality, insofar as rationality operates on the foundation of fairness.

I am contending, then, that the original position forces one to see one's own self-interest as identical with that of all other people. In this sense, perhaps it would be helpful to think of the original position as the neutral position. The term is useful since it can suggest an act of neutralizing or putting out of play certain tendencies and information. In a neutral position one neither denies nor affirms certain facts about people; one simply makes no use of these facts, so that as a result there is neither a self for whose interests nor against whose interests one could choose. In this connection, Husserl's reduction again comes to mind.

The priority of the good is irrational not because one would in this way be acting against one's own self-interest, but because the original position, by *subjugating* self-interest, has made the *common* nature of the person the proper basis for choosing principles of justice. Thanks to the fairness doctrine, this is the way in which *anyone* must reason if he is to reason fairly about justice. An original position doctrine is therefore the vehicle for moving people into a moral point of view which is nearly impossible to adopt simply on the basis of the moral value of impartiality.[32] For impartiality, like justice itself, has normally been brought to bear upon an already constituted set of facts about which one is then to become impartial or toward which one is to adopt the just attitude. But the question is whether it is humanly possible to be truly impartial when, operating on the basis of full information, one necessarily knows the facts as well as one's point of view on them. The vicissitudes of the history of impartiality in law and justice would suggest a negative answer. This is the reason why it is so valuable to employ the fictional device of an original position. By objectifying its members outside of ourselves, as it were, we can "observe" their processes of decision in a pure state. We can ask ourselves what "they" would do on the basis of fairness and the information provided them. Of course, we must remember that "they" do not really exist but remain our fictional constructs. But in an important sense we are the deliberators of the original position. We are interested in what they will do and choose because they represent us at our very best. Men as natural beings cannot be just if justice cannot be found in the natural world. But if we look elsewhere, away from our aims and the good, there is every chance that we may be on the right path toward justice and a conception of freedom which respects the profound nature of moral personality.

Thus the argument of this paper supports freedom as a value in its own right, consisting precisely in its independence of other values. Freedom is an absolute value in the sense that it is the condition *sine qua non* of a human life. But insofar as the exercise of freedom must be judged by the criteria of the right, it is a relative value; individual liberty is *limited* by what is right and just, not by what is good. Importantly, the foregoing analysis has tried to show that, quite apart from the goodness or badness of its objects, freedom has a value and is worth preserving even when its objects are not worth preserving.[33] This is why it is impossible to judge freedom first and foremost in terms of the good. We may readily agree that a totalitarian political regime or a theocracy could well produce social peace and saintly lives, as well as many other values and expressions of the good. But no achievement, however great, is ever worth the price of dismantling the moral basis of personhood, not even worth disturbing the sanctity of a single conscience. Whether circumstances or natural necessities may sometimes force us to pay that price is another question. And, given our natural interest in other human values, such as peace, security, and social stability, circumstances may often prompt us voluntarily to limit our freedom for the sake of other values. Thus, in the last analysis, the basic issues cannot really be drawn so sharply. We must ask: Which is *more* important, the moral personality of human beings or the aims and goals which they pursue?[34] To emphasize one at the complete expense of the other would be foolhardy. So it is a question of priority, and Rawls, I believe, has given an uncommonly profound defense of the correct priority.[35]

NOTES

1. John Rawls, *A Theory of Justice* (Cambridge: The Belknap Press of Harvard University Press, 1971).

2. This emphasis may be especially pertinent in the light of major themes found in the articles by Norris Clarke, Joseph Dolan, and Gerald McCool in this volume. Clarke, for example, seems to argue the case for the priority of the good and the subordination of freedom to the good. By contrast, Rawls argues the case for the subordination of freedom and the good to the right.

3. For a recent collection of essays which critically assess various aspects of *A Theory of Justice* from philosophic, legal, and social scientific perspectives, see *Reading Rawls: Critical Studies on Rawls'* A THEORY OF JUSTICE, ed. Norman Daniels (New York: Basic Books, 1975).

4. This is Hutcheson's formulation in *An Inquiry Concerning Moral Good and Evil* (1725), cited in Rawls, *A Theory of Justice*, p. 22n9.

5. See ibid., pp. 24–25: "It is natural to think that rationality is maximizing something and that in morals it must be maximizing the good."

6. According to Rawls, "Utilitarianism does not take seriously the distinc-

tion between persons" (ibid., p. 27). Nor, on the other hand, does utilitarianism take seriously their involvement in each other's nature. See ibid., section 79, "The Idea of Social Union," pp. 520–29.

7. William K. Frankena, *Ethics*, 2nd ed. (Englewood Cliffs: Prentice-Hall, 1973), p. 14.

8. Frankena is not clear on why the source of moral obligation cannot be a moral value. He suggests that for moral obligation to depend on the moral value of what it promotes is circular (ibid.). But it is not clear why this should be the case.

9. Norris Clarke's article in this volume might be said to be an excellent example of the deep appeal of a teleological theory. Thus he says: "It is precisely because, and only because, of this essential subordination of freedom to the good, i.e., to the goodness of the order of ends, that our intrinsic rights to the exercise of freedom can be limited and restricted. . . ." This is a perfect example of what Rawls is opposed to, the priority of the good. Beginning with such a powerful idea of the good, the right is, from a Rawlsian perspective, effectively overshadowed.

10. Again, the contrast with Norris Clarke's analysis is very striking. Clarke seems to be saying that one can be free for something only because we are first necessitated to something. He holds that because "we are permanently magnetized by the deepest necessity of our nature toward the Infinite Good," we are "able to be free . . . toward any and all finite goods along the way to this one ultimate and final Goal." Compare Rawls's discussion of "Happiness and Dominant Ends" in *A Theory of Justice*, pp. 548–54.

11. Frankena, *Ethics*, p. 15.

12. *A Theory of Justice*, p. 30. See also p. 477, where Rawls gives grounds for rejecting the doctrine of the purely conscientious act.

13. Ibid., p. 560.

14. Rawls is not a party to skepticism or relativism, or a casualty of theoretical desperation in matters of epistemology and metaphysics. See his discussion of the grounds for equal liberty of conscience and toleration in chap. 4 of *A Theory of Justice* and his "The Independence of Moral Theory," *Proceedings and Addresses of the American Philosophical Association*, 48 (1974–75), 5–22.

15. One is not exactly forced to guess the applicability of Rawls's ideas to contemporary social institutions, but Rawls is not polemical or critical; nor is he in an ivory tower. See Thomas Nagel's remarks at the end of his "Rawls on Justice," in *Reading Rawls*, ed. Daniels, p. 16: "The outlook expressed by this book is not characteristic of its age, for it is neither pessimistic nor alienated nor angry nor sentimental nor utopian. Instead it conveys something that today may seem incredible: a hopeful affirmation of human possibilities."

16. Much of *A Theory of Justice* is of course concerned with how to deal with the inequalities of nature and society and the effects which such inequalities have on our liberties. For a discussion of Rawls's distinction between equal liberty and the worth of liberty, see Norman Daniels, "Equal Liberty and Unequal Worth of Liberty," ibid., pp. 253–81.

17. Rawls gives a compelling, perhaps a quasi-independent, justification for a good part of his conception of justice by assessing traditional theories of justice in

terms of the arbitrariness of their principles. See *A Theory of Justice*, pp. 65–75, where Rawls's theory would seem to be the next logical step in the evolution of justice as it progressively sheds arbitrariness.

18. I have not touched on the nature of Rawls's theory of the good ("Goodness as Rationality") and I shall not discuss it in this paper. In speaking of his "key position on the good," I am not referring to his positive statements on the nature of the good but rather emphasizing the negative side, the freedom from the good or the priority-of-the-right position. A full sketch of his work would have to say a great deal about his theory of the good.

19. See *A Theory of Justice*, section 14, "Fair Equality of Opportunity and Pure Procedural Justice," esp. pp. 85–86.

20. Ibid., p. 86.

21. Ibid., p. 120.

22. Ibid., p. 554.

23. Ibid., section 79, "The Idea of Social Union," pp. 520–29.

24. See Victor Gourevitch, "Rawls on Justice," *The Review of Metaphysics*, 28, No. 3, Issue No. 111 (March 1975), 501.

25. At the outset of *A Theory of Justice*, Rawls asserts that a conception of justice derives from a conception of society, "a vision of the way in which the aims and purposes of social cooperation are to be understood" (p. 9). His vision of society is contained in "The Idea of Social Union" (pp. 520–29), which argues that members of a community participate in one another's nature. It is one of the few places in *A Theory of Justice* where one can see almost explicit criticism of Marxism. Rawls's conception of society as a social union may also be helpful in explaining his differences with the position of Robert Nozick's *Anarchy, State and Utopia* (New York: Basic Books, 1974), which seems to derive from a radically individualistic conception of human nature.

26. See *A Theory of Justice*, section 50, "The Principle of Perfection," pp. 325–32.

27. See, for example, Joel Feinberg, *Social Philosophy* (Englewood Cliffs: Prentice-Hall, 1973), p. 6.

28. See Emmanuel Levinas, *Totality and Infinity* (Pittsburgh: Duquesne University Press, 1969) for an interpretation of various philosophies and ontologies which contain this impulse.

29. See the second part of Kant's essay "On the Common Saying: 'This may be True in Theory, but it does not Apply in Practice,'" *Kant's Political Writings*, ed. Hans Reiss (Cambridge: Cambridge University Press, 1970), pp. 73–74.

30. The nature and implications of Rawls's notion of primary goods can be a fairly controversial subject. But I cannot go into the issues here. For a view of one apparent problem, however, see Thomas Nagel, "Rawls on Justice," pp. 9–10. For Rawls's rejoinder, see the article cited in note 34.

31. For a criticism of rationality which is defined in terms of "safety-first prudentialism," and which indirectly bears on Rawls's own view of rationality, see Nicholas Rescher, *Unselfishness: The Role of the Vicarious Affects in Moral Philosophy and Social Theory* (Pittsburgh: The University of Pittsburgh Press, 1975).

32. It may be that the concept of impartiality (unlike the conditions of the

original position) necessarily implies personal access to full information. Judges and referees, for example, must know all the relevant facts before making an impartial decision. In practice, this ideal often amounts to showing no discernible evidence of favoritism in deciding an issue, and hindsight alone may reveal the bias which full information allowed. Brian Barry presents a contrary view. He maintains that "there is not a great deal of practical difference between invoking Rawls's 'veil of ignorance' and simply demanding that an 'ideal observer' should behave impartially, or saying that people's moral judgments are more likely to be unprejudiced if their own interests are not at stake in the matter under discussion" (*The Liberal Theory of Justice* [Oxford: Clarendon, 1973], p. 12). Yet the crucial question is how to implement the ideal of impartiality under conditions of full information.

33. See Robert Neville, *The Cosmology of Freedom* (New Haven: Yale University Press, 1974), p. 286: "[T]he subjective value of choosing is worth prizing even when the objective values produced are not. In fact, it is worth prizing even when the objective values are far worse than alternatives that could have been chosen or imposed from without." So too, some things, certain forms of behavior, for example, may be just even though it may be difficult or impossible to endorse them in terms of standards of goodness. See Rawls, *A Theory of Justice*, pp. 331, 424–33.

34. See Rawls, "Fairness to Goodness," *The Philosophical Review*, 84 (1975), 536–54, at 554: "We should not speak of fairness to conceptions of the good, but of fairness to moral persons. . . . [I]t is fairness to persons that is primary and not fairness to conceptions of the good as such." (The present essay was already completed when the above article appeared. Among other things, it clarifies several points concerning objections to his account of "primary goods" and certain features of the original position. In light of this article I would now discuss certain additional points and add or subtract a few emphases. But on the whole I believe his new remarks on the problem of goodness do not greatly affect the substance of my essay.)

35. I am indebted to Donald Campion, John McNaughton, and Clyde Walton for comments on an earlier version of this paper.